CONFIRMATION
IN THE APOSTOLIC AGE

CONFIRMATION
IN THE APOSTOLIC AGE

BY

FREDERIC HENRY CHASE,
D.D., Hon. D.D. (Oxon.)
Bishop of Ely

WIPF & STOCK · Eugene, Oregon

Wipf and Stock Publishers
199 W 8th Ave, Suite 3
Eugene, OR 97401

Confirmation in the Apostolic Age
By Chase, F. H.
ISBN 13: 978-1-60608-332-1
Publication date 2/17/2016
Previously published by Macmillan & Co., 1909

TO

HENRY BARCLAY SWETE D.D.

REGIUS PROFESSOR OF DIVINITY CAMBRIDGE

WITH

THE GRATITUDE

AND AFFECTIONATE REGARD

OF A FORMER COLLEAGUE

PREFACE

FEW words only are needed to explain the origin of this short Essay. Some years ago when I was Principal of the Clergy Training School, Cambridge, I used to lecture to the members of the School on Christian Doctrine ; and part of the course on the Sacraments was devoted to the subject of Confirmation. If this book should chance to fall into the hands of any of my old pupils and friends of those days, they may perhaps be reminded of what was a happy and useful time to me and I should like to think to them also. When it became my duty and happiness as Bishop to minister Confirmation, I naturally for my own guidance and help reviewed under a new sense of responsibility what I had written on Confirmation in former years. On several occasions I have lectured on Confirmation to meetings of Clergy; and from time to time I have been asked to publish the substance of the lectures. This little volume is a response to these requests. It will be no ordinary pleasure if I am allowed in this way to help my brethren the parochial Clergy in their own study of the subject and in their most important work of preparing Candidates for the Laying on of Hands.

In working at the subject and in putting my notes in order for publication I have avoided consulting any of the many books on Confirmation, nor have I passed beyond the limits of the New Testament. The conclusions as to the teaching of the New Testament, which I have thus reached independently of others, are, I believe, strongly confirmed by the fact that in the belief of the Church of the first centuries the gift given to the true disciple in Confirmation is the gift of the Holy Spirit.

In the revision of the proof sheets I have had the help of a younger student of

PREFACE

theology. He knows at least in part what a very peculiar pleasure it is to me to thank him for his criticisms and suggestions.

I must confess that, when I was a young clergyman, my views as to Confirmation were vague. Clearness and definiteness came to me from one to whom I with numberless others owe a debt which we can never express in words. The first year I examined for the Theological Tripos in Cambridge was the last year Dr Westcott examined. I vividly remember the meeting of examiners for the review of the examination papers held in Dr Westcott's house in Scroope Terrace one day in May 1886. We worked from early morning till late afternoon at our somewhat dreary task of criticism and revision. But there was an oasis in the desert. The examiner who set the paper on Christian Doctrine gave some patristic passages for comment. Among these was one from Tertullian's treatise *de Baptismo* vi.—' Non quod in aquis Spiritum Sanctum consequamur, sed in aqua emundati sub angelo Spiritui Sancto praeparamur.' The subject was clearly one on which Dr Westcott had a definite and strong conviction. For a few moments he spoke, as those who knew him can imagine him speaking, on the true meaning of Confirmation suggested by Tertullian's words. 'If,' I remember that he said, 'Confirmation had been always properly understood, many of the controversies about Baptism would never have arisen.' Dr Westcott's words were always strangely illuminating. To his words of that afternoon I look back with abiding gratitude.

CONTENTS

CONTENTS

CONTENTS

CONFIRMATION IN THE APOSTOLIC AGE

I propose in the following pages to review the evidence which the New Testament supplies as to the place of Confirmation during the Apostolic age in the life and thought of the Church. I shall endeavour to consider the passages of the Apostolic writings which refer, or may be reasonably thought to refer, to Confirmation. The subsequent history of Confirmation in the Church of Christ lies outside the range of this investigation. I shall indeed have occasion to speak of the Confirmation Service in the Book of Common Prayer both in its present and in its earlier forms. Otherwise I shall hardly transgress the limits of the New Testament.

The attempt, however inadequately carried out, to gain a clear conception of the thoughts which in the first days gathered round an Ordinance of the Church can never be without profit. Custom, routine, and controversy had not as yet marred the first freshness and simplicity of faith. The essential meaning of the primary rites of the Church was not as yet obscured by the influence of secondary and accidental associations. The sense of the powers of the spiritual world was vivid and immediate. The conscious effort therefore to bring ourselves into contact with this age of initial inspiration cannot but tend to correct and to quicken our use of the inheritance which is ours as members of Christ's Church. Much indeed of the ground which is traversed in the following pages has often been traversed before. Yet, as we pass along, some of the details which will claim our attention may be fresh wholly or in part. Of such a subject it is always worth while to endeavour to gain a connected view.

The two great *momenta* of the whole Christian dispensation are (1) the Incarnation of the Son of God; (2) the outpouring of the Holy Spirit of God. In that whole dispensation the divine purpose in the creation of man in the image of God and with a capacity to attain to the likeness of God was ideally fulfilled; and, to use the bold phrase of Greek theology, man was put into the way of 'being made divine' (θεοποιεῖσθαι).

The purpose of the Incarnation was threefold—revelation, reconciliation, fellowship. The Son came in the Father's Name (*e.g.* John v. 43) and revealed the Father to men (*e.g.* John xiv. 9, xvii. 26). Through the atoning life and death of the Incarnate Son of God man was cleansed, forgiven, reconciled to God; through the Lord's quickening resurrection man 'was begotten again unto a living hope' (1 Pet. i. 3): 'in Christ' man is the redeemed son of the Father in Heaven. 'In Christ' man can 'abide in God and God in him' (1 John iv. 16).

The purpose of the outpouring of the Holy Spirit also was threefold—revelation, endowment, fellowship. As the Son was sent in the Father's Name and revealed the Father, so the Spirit was sent in the Son's Name (John xiv. 26) and reveals the Son (John xv. 26, xvi. 14). Through the power of the indwelling Spirit each member of the Church is taught little by little to understand the infinite meaning of the Incarnation, and with a faith which grows larger and deeper to believe in the Lord Jesus Christ. Through the power of the indwelling Spirit the manifold gifts of grace are communicated to all those who are 'in Christ'—faith, wisdom, knowledge, 'a right judgment in all things.' Through the power of the indwelling Spirit the divine blessing of 'fellowship' is realized by each of the faithful (2 Cor. xiii. 13, Phil. ii. 1), the fellowship of man with the Father and with the Son (1 John i. 3), the fellowship of man with man in the brotherhood of the redeemed (1 John i. 7 ; comp. Eph. iv. 3 ff.).

These two great *momenta* of the whole Christian dispensation, the Incarnation of the Son of God and the outpouring of the Spirit of God, are brought into contact with the individual in Baptism and in Confirmation.

It is no objection against this position to say that the truths connected with the Incarnation and the gift of the Spirit may be, and often are, vitally apprehended at some other time than the season of Baptism and the season of Confirmation. As we trace the divine action we see that God has been pleased to deal with the world by historical events. We might *a priori* have expected that God would have wrought out the spiritual work of redemption by a spiritual process in the spirits of men. We know that He did redeem the world by a series of historical events which took their place among other historical events. These events were at the time only very partially understood even by the holiest men who watched them and had their part in them. The disciples did not at once grasp the meaning of the Lord's life on earth or of the Cross or of the Resurrection or of Pentecost. But there were the events, complete on the divine side, perfect manifestations of the eternal will of God, for the mind and the heart to work upon,

5

for men gradually to realize and to appropriate. And as it was with the world, so it is with the individual.

Baptism is the sacrament of cleansing. The first Christian act done to the little child is an act of washing. He is thereby outwardly, visibly, historically brought into contact with ' the redemption which is in Christ Jesus.' He must 'lead the rest of his life according to this beginning.' We confess 'one Baptism for the remission of sins.' Baptism is both the pledge of forgiveness and an assured entrance into a new life in which forgiveness and cleansing are essential and abiding elements. ' If we walk in the light...the blood of Jesus his Son cleanseth us from all sin' (1 John i. 7).

Baptism is the sacrament of regeneration. It is the revelation of the divine Fatherhood in the case of the individual life. It is as though God laid His hand on the baptised and said ' This is my son,' 'This is my daughter.' The fact of Fatherhood on God's side and of sonship on man's cannot be altered. It remains a fact, a source of untold blessing or a seal of condemnation. It must in daily life be recognised and realized. He who has proved himself unworthy to be called a son of God must return and claim that which is his with the confession 'Father, I have sinned.' Conversion is based on regeneration. Again, as in the natural so in the spiritual world birth is a beginning; it is not maturity. Birth must be followed by growth and development. And growth and development depend on the healthfulness of the conditions of life. Regeneration is not spiritual attainment.

Baptism is the sacrament of incorporation. He who is baptised is baptised 'into Jesus Christ.' He is brought into union with Christ and, through Christ the Mediator, into union with the Father and with the Spirit (Matt. xxviii. 19). But in this aspect also Baptism is a beginning. He who has been baptised into Christ 'must grow up in all things into Him' (Eph. iv. 15). Union must become communion. The union with Christ which is pledged in Baptism is confirmed and deepened in the Eucharist. The divine Presence vouchsafed to the believer in the Eucharist can only be rightly understood in the light of the divine Presence assured to him in Baptism.

Baptism then is the impartment outwardly, visibly, historically, of the new life in Christ. But in the spiritual order there can be no life apart from that Holy Spirit who is 'the Giver of life.' In Baptism the Holy Spirit works and is bestowed as the divine Power who quickens and renews.

In Confirmation the redeemed child of the Heavenly Father is outwardly, visibly, historically brought into contact with the second great *momentum* of the whole Christian dispensation. In Confirmation he is made a partaker of the Holy Spirit— the Spirit of revelation, unfolding to him according to the measure of his growing capacity the fulness of the Incarnate Word; the Spirit of endowment, communicating to him the manifold grace of God that he may live and serve according to the Father's will; the Spirit of fellowship, bringing him into closer union and communion with God and with man. Confirmation is the strengthening of the child of God by the Father's gift of the Father's Spirit[1].

[1] It seems to me a most serious loss when in the Confirmation

In the Sacraments[1] it is the divine side, that which God gives to man, which is essential. Everything else is secondary and subordinate, it may be of great spiritual beauty and value, of great importance in the sphere of Church order and of practical edification, but not the very thing itself which is the intention of the Sacrament. But among Christian men there has been ever a tendency to exalt the human and secondary element in the Sacrament, to give undue prominence (1) in Baptism to the promises made by the Catechumen or by the Sponsors ; (2) in the Eucharist to the memorial before God made by man of the Sacrifice completed on the Cross ; (3) in Confirmation to the renewal of the promises

prayer 'Defend, O Lord, this thy Child,' the word 'Servant' is substituted for the word 'Child.' We do not cease to be God's children when we grow old. The oldest no less than the youngest candidate for Confirmation seeks the divine gift as the redeemed child of God ; compare Gal. iv. 6 'Because ye are sons, God sent forth the Spirit of his Son into our hearts.' In any revision of the Prayer Book we may hope that the alternative phrase 'Or this thy Servant' will be struck out.

[1] I have ventured to use the word Sacrament in an extended sense so as to include Confirmation. The 'outward and visible sign' in Confirmation, the laying on of hands, has the clear authority of the New Testament, though we have no explicit declaration in the New Testament that it was 'ordained by Christ Himself.'

made at Baptism. It is with this last point alone that we are now concerned.

The ratification of the baptismal vows was in days not long past generally regarded, and is still too often regarded, as the chief meaning of Confirmation. The phraseology of the Book of Common Prayer is doubtless largely responsible for this popular misconception. It is worth while therefore to trace the history of this phraseology; for it is not too much to hope that in any revision of the Book it may be rectified. In the rubrics then which in the First Prayer Book of Edward VI. (1549) preface the service it is said, 'And this order is most convenient to be observed for divers considerations. First, because that when children come to the years of discretion, and have learned what their Godfathers and Godmothers promised for them in Baptism, they may then with their own mouth, and with their own consent, ratify and confess the same.' In the Second Prayer Book of Edward VI. (1552) these rubrics kept the place which they had in the First Book, but (possibly through a mere printer's error or more probably from a love of verbal conceits[1]) the word 'confirm' was substituted for the word 'confess.' In the Prayer Book of 1662 the rubrics of the two older Books became the Preface to be read by the Bishop 'or some other Minister appointed by him'; and in the Preface, in spite of the obvious tautology, the phrase 'ratify and confirm' was retained; and there to the confusion of our people's minds it still remains. Further, in 1662 the question of the Bishop and the answer of those to be Confirmed were added; and in that question the language of the Preface reappears, 'ratifying and confirming the same in your own persons.' Thus the words 'ratify and confirm,' 'ratifying and confirming,' standing in the very forefront of the service, appear to give an authoritative interpretation of the name of the rite—Confirmation. They suggest that the meaning of Confirmation is not that those who have been baptised are therein them-

---

[1] When it is said, as it is often said, that the Candidate 'confirms and is confirmed,' the word 'confirm' is used in two wholly different connotations. There is no real analogy between 'confirming (ratifying) promises' and 'being confirmed (strengthened) by the gift of the Spirit.'

selves confirmed by the gift of the Spirit, but that they confirm the promises once made for them by their Godparents. And this impression, conveyed by the actual language of the service, is strengthened by the absence of the word 'confirm' in the prayer at the laying on of hands and in the other prayers. The older Books were not open to this charge. In the Prayer Book of 1549 and in that of 1552 the rubric immediately preceding the actual service was 'And the Bishop shall confirm them on this wise[1]'; and in the former of these two Books the prayer which the 'Minister' said before the Bishop's act of Confirmation contained the petition addressed to God 'Confirm and strength them with the inward unction of thy Holy Ghost.' Thus the use of the word 'confirm' by the Prayer Book of 1662 in the one context and its omission in the other have together facilitated a fatal lowering of the conception of Confirmation. The emphasis of the Service

[1] In the present 'Order of Confirmation' we have in the first rubric 'all that are to be then confirmed'; in the Preface 'none hereafter shall be confirmed'; in the final rubric 'until such time as he be confirmed, or be ready and desirous to be confirmed.'

appears to rest on the human, not on the divine side. The essence of the rite lies in the prayer for the gift of the Spirit and in the laying on of hands (comp. Acts viii. 15, 17). The renewal of the Baptismal vows on the other hand is an accident of the rite, appropriate only in the case of those whose Confirmation is separated from their Baptism by an interval of time. It is the pledge on the part of those who were baptised in infancy and who in riper years present themselves for Confirmation that they are fit to receive the outward and visible sign of so great an inward and spiritual grace[1].

[1] The Preface and the Question in the Order of Confirmation, if I may frankly express my own opinion, are in urgent need of complete revision. (1) It must be confessed that the Preface is frigid and stiff to an even painful degree. Its history explains its character. It is a rubric made to serve a purpose for which it was not originally intended. It is not an address to the Candidates but a formal and impersonal statement of the conditions of Confirmation. We can hardly therefore wonder that it is wholly destitute of spiritual power or fervour, and stands in complete contrast to the Exhortations in the Communion Office, to the Addresses in the Baptismal Offices, and to the Address in the Ordinal to Candidates for the Priesthood. (2) It is a Preface not to the Service but only to the Question. It does not say a single word as to the essential meaning of Confirmation, an omission which is an unspeakable loss. The Service of Confirmation is a deeply significant Service both to the Candidates themselves and also to the general congregation. Is it not the bounden duty of the Church to set forth with authority in that

In approaching the teaching of the New Testament on the subject of Confirmation let us consider two analogies.

(1) There is the analogy between God's historical dealings with His Son and His historical dealings with us. The Lord as the representative Israelite chose to have part in the Baptism of His forerunner. He was baptised by John in the river Jordan. As He came up out of the water, the Spirit descended upon Him. The Lord's Baptism was followed by the Lord's Confirmation. He was confirmed by His Father through the Holy Spirit. Throughout His earthly life He could look back

Service the spiritual gift in Confirmation, and that in words which will touch hearts and consciences? (3) A Bishop who has the happiness of confirming many adult and sometimes aged persons cannot but feel keenly the inappropriateness of the Preface in such cases. Its language—'that children being now come to years of discretion'—suggests that Confirmation is a rite only for the young, and thus increases the difficulty which older persons often experience in offering themselves for this means of grace. (4) It is obvious that the Preface and the Question are applicable only in the case of those who were baptised in infancy and who had sponsors. Under the conditions of the present day when many come forward for Confirmation who were baptised in infancy by a Nonconformist Minister or who were baptised as adults, perhaps immediately before Confirmation, some change is clearly necessary. It is most important that Candidates should give a pledge of fitness; but such a pledge ought not to take a form which is untrue and unreal in the case of a considerable number.

to that hour as the time when, and to that
place as the place where, He received the
fulness of the Father's gift. We note in
the history the immediate connexion between the Baptism, the outpouring of the
Spirit, and the assurance of Sonship.
Herein the Lord set an example to all
His disciples. The disciple may well be
content to do and to receive what the
Master Himself did and received. In this
history we have a sufficient argument for
Confirmation.

The sequel is well worth attentive
study. We can trace at least in part the
different offices which the Holy Spirit
fulfilled to the Son of Man.

The Spirit was to the Lord the Spirit
of guidance and support in conflict.
'Jesus, full of the Holy Spirit, returned
from the Jordan, and was led by the Spirit
in the wilderness during forty days, being
tempted of the devil' (Luke iv. 1)[1]. The

---

[1] ἤγετο ἐν τῷ πνεύματι ἐν τῇ ἐρήμῳ ἡμέρας τεσσεράκοντα πειραζόμενος ὑπὸ τοῦ διαβόλου. The true reading ἐν τῇ ἐρήμῳ (not
εἰς τὴν ἔρημον) contains a gospel of hope. Note the two coincident
and continuous experiences (ἤγετο, πειραζόμενος). In Westcott
and Hort's text ἤγετο...ἐν τῇ ἐρήμῳ should be printed as a quota-
tion in uncials : the words are derived from Deut. viii. 2 ἤγαγέν

guidance was continuous, unbroken by the stress of conflict. 'Led by the Spirit,' 'tempted of the devil'—such was the two-fold experience of the incarnate Son of God; such is the twofold experience of every true Christian.

The Spirit was to the Lord the Spirit of strength. 'Jesus returned in the power of the Spirit into Galilee' (Luke iv. 14).

The Spirit was to the Lord the Spirit of ministry. The Lord applied to Himself the words of the Prophet 'The Spirit of the Lord is upon me, because he anointed me to preach good tidings to the poor' (Luke iv. 18 ; Is. lxi. 1).

The Spirit was to the Lord the Spirit of discernment. He after His Resurrection 'gave commandment unto the Apostles whom through the Holy Spirit he had chosen' (Acts i. 2)[1].

σε Κύριος ὁ θεός σου ἐν τῇ ἐρήμῳ (v. 3 contains the Lord's answer to the first temptation). Comp. Gal. v. 18, Rom. viii. 14 ὅσοι γὰρ πνεύματι θεοῦ ἄγονται, οὗτοι υἱοὶ θεοῦ εἰσίν.

[1] Such I believe to be the true interpretation of St Luke's words : ἄχρι ἧς ἡμέρας ἐντειλάμενος τοῖς ἀποστόλοις διὰ πνεύματος ἁγίου οὓς ἐξελέξατο ἀνελήμφθη. The words διὰ πνεύματος ἁγίου are emphatic by their position and thus connect with the Apostles' first selection the history of their reception of the Spirit and of their life and activity in the Spirit.

The Spirit was to the Lord the Spirit of revelation. 'He whom God sent speaketh the words of God; for not by measure giveth he the Spirit' (John iii. 34).

The Spirit was to the Lord the Spirit of victory. 'If I by the Spirit of God cast out devils' (Matt. xii. 28).

The Spirit was to the Lord the Spirit of joy. Jesus 'exalted in the Holy Spirit and said I thank thee, O Father, Lord of heaven and earth' (Luke x. 21)[1].

The Spirit was to the Lord the Spirit of sacrifice. 'The Christ...through the eternal Spirit offered himself without blemish to God' (Hebr. ix. 14)[2].

---

[1] The true text is ἠγαλλιάσατο τῷ πνεύματι τῷ ἁγίῳ. Comp. 1 Thess. i. 6, Gal. v. 22.

[2] There are two controverted points in these words; see the notes of Bp Westcott and Dr Vaughan. (a) The reference in προσήνεγκεν is, I believe, not to Christ's 'self-presentation as the risen and ascended Lord in heaven itself' but to the sacrifice consummated on the Cross; comp. ix. 28, x. 12. This reference seems to me to be required by the word ἄμωμον. (b) Bishop Westcott takes the words διὰ πνεύματος αἰωνίου to refer to *Christ's* Spirit. 'Christ's Spirit,' he says, 'is in virtue of His Divine Personality eternal.' The 'Spirit is to be regarded as the seat of His Divine Personality in His human Nature.' It is true that πνεῦμα, a synonym (when contrasted with σάρξ) of the term λόγος, is used by some early Christian writers to denote the Divine Nature of the Incarnate Son; *e.g.* [Clem. Rom.] ii. 9 ὢν τὸ μὲν πρῶτον πνεῦμα ἐγένετο σάρξ. But this use of πνεῦμα

The Spirit was to the Lord the Spirit of resurrection and life. Jesus 'was declared to be the Son of God with power, according to the Spirit of holiness, by the resurrection of the dead' (Rom. i. 4)[1].

What the Spirit of the Father was to the incarnate Son on earth, that He will be to all who through the Son are children of God.

(2) There is the analogy between God's historical dealing with the Church

---

has no support in the N.T. If then it is meant that Christ's human spirit is here referred to, then it must be urged that Christ's human spirit was *a parte ante* no more eternal than His human body. We are brought therefore to the simplest, and (as it appears) the necessary, interpretation of the words, viz. that by them is meant the Holy Spirit. The epithet αἰωνίου connects the historical act in time with the eternal purpose and will. Through the presence and cooperation of the Spirit the Lord was enabled to 'become obedient unto death'; and further through that same presence and cooperation, as He was guided and supported in the wilderness of temptation, so He remained to the end ἄμωμος. It should be added that the absence of the article (διὰ πνεύματος αἰωνίου) does not make the words in any sense indefinite but fixes attention on character—'through Him who is Spirit and Eternal'; see Additional Note.

[1] κατὰ πνεῦμα ἁγιωσύνης. This is the one instance in the New Testament of the exact translation of the Semitic phrase, 'Spirit of holiness,' 'Spirit of His holiness,' found in Ps. li. 11, Is. lxiii. 11, and universal in the Syriac versions of the N.T. For the thought comp. Rom. viii. 11 εἰ δὲ τὸ πνεῦμα τοῦ ἐγείραντος τὸν Ἰησοῦν ἐκ νεκρῶν οἰκεῖ ἐν ὑμῖν, ὁ ἐγείρας ἐκ νεκρῶν Χριστὸν Ἰησοῦν ζωοποιήσει καὶ τὰ θνητὰ σώματα ὑμῶν διὰ τοῦ ἐνοικοῦντος αὐτοῦ πνεύματος (v.l. διὰ τὸ ἐνοικοῦν αὐτοῦ πνεῦμα) ἐν ὑμῖν.

and God's historical dealing with individuals. During the time of the Lord's ministry the Church may be said to have been in the position of a catechumen. The Lord was commonly known as 'the teacher,' His followers as 'His disciples,' 'His scholars.' It was the period of the Church's preparatory training. The day of the Resurrection, not (as is often said) the day of Pentecost, was the Church's birthday. When the Lord rose from the dead, the Church, 'the first fruits unto God' from among men, came into being. On the evening of 'that day, the first day of the week,' the risen Lord appeared to the representatives of the Church, the Eleven and 'them that were with them' (John xx. 19, Luke xxiv. 33). He 'breathed on them,' a sacramental act significant of a new creation[1]. He said to them 'Receive ye the Holy Ghost,' the

---

[1] John xx. 22 καὶ τοῦτο εἰπὼν ἐνεφύσησεν καὶ λέγει αὐτοῖς, Λάβετε πνεῦμα ἅγιον. Comp. Gen. ii. 7 ἐνεφύσησεν εἰς τὸ πρόσωπον αὐτοῦ πνοὴν ζωῆς καὶ ἐγένετο ὁ ἄνθρωπος εἰς ψυχὴν ζῶσαν. I Kings xvii. 21 καὶ ἐνεφύσησεν τῷ παιδαρίῳ τρίς. Ezek. xxxvii. 9 ἐλθὲ καὶ ἐμφύσησον εἰς τοὺς νεκροὺς τούτους καὶ ζησάτωσαν. Wisd. xv. 11 τὸν ἐμπνεύσαντα αὐτῷ ψυχὴν ἐνεργοῦσαν καὶ ἐμφυσήσαντα πνεῦμα ζωτικόν.

quickening Spirit. By His act and by His words He made the Church partaker of His own risen life.

The Church then on the first Easter day came into being. The Church's birthday was succeeded by a time of waiting. In the brief interval between Easter and Pentecost the historian places one event, the choice of St Matthias. The Church lived. Action is the sign of life; and the Church acted. But in that action there is no thought of spiritual direction, no trust in an inspiration of right judgment. The disciples sought for guidance through the earthly and mechanical expedient of casting lots. The one action recorded in those days was an action marked by spiritual immaturity.

The time of waiting came to an end. Then on a definite day, the day of Pentecost; at a definite hour in the early morning of that day; in a definite place, the Temple, the Father 'poured forth' on the representatives of the redeemed Church the gift of the Holy Ghost. Henceforth the Church is the 'Spirit-bearing Body.' The day of Pentecost was the day of the Church's

Confirmation. Confirmation is the Pentecost of the individual soul[1].

The analogy between the stages of the life of the whole Christian Society and the stages of the life of the individual member of that Society is complete.

We now turn to those passages of the New Testament which refer, or which may be thought to refer, to Confirmation. They fall into three groups: (1) the historical passages of the Book of the Acts; (2) passages of the Apostolic Epistles which speak of an outward and visible sign and of the corresponding inward and spiritual grace; (3) passages of the Apostolic Epistles which speak of the definite reception of the gift of the Holy Spirit.

[1] (1) I cannot doubt that the place where the Apostles received the Spirit was the Temple. As at the Passover so at Pentecost it was the custom that the Priests should open the gates of the Temple at midnight, and that the crowds of worshippers should wait in the Temple courts for the solemnities of the Feast (see Edersheim, *The Temple*, pp. 228 ff.). The Apostles, like other devout Jews, would naturally resort to the Temple 'when the day of Pentecost was being fulfilled.' If the scene of the history

I. *The historical passages of the Book of the Acts.*

The history of the Christian Church contained in the Book of the Acts is articulated by the words of the Risen Lord recorded by St Luke (Acts i. 8): 'Ye shall be my witnesses both in Jerusalem, and in all Judaea[1] and Samaria, and unto the

---

was the Temple, we have an explanation of what otherwise appears to be inexplicable, *i.e.* (*a*) of the presence of large numbers of Jews of the Dispersion (Acts ii. 9 ff.); (*b*) of the possibility of so vast a crowd coming together and listening to St Peter's words. The language of the historian completely harmonizes with this view: (i) ἦσαν ἐπὶ τὸ αὐτό (*v.* 1) implies assembling for worship (comp. 1 Cor. xi. 20, xiv. 23; Clem. Rom. xxxiv. 7, Ign. *Philad.* VI. 2); (ii) οἶκος (*v.* 2) is the regular term in the LXX. (*e.g.* Jer. xlii. (xxxv.) 4) and in Josephus (*e.g. Antiq.* VII. xiv. 10) for one of the chambers of the Temple; (iii) τὸ πλῆθος (*v.* 6) is elsewhere used by St Luke (Luke i. 10, Acts xxi. 36) of the crowd of worshippers in the Temple Courts.

(2) ἐκχεῶ (*v.* 17; Joel ii. 28 (iii. 1)) is the Pentecostal keyword; see *v.* 33, x. 45, Tit. iii. 6; comp. Zech. xii. 10 ἐκχεῶ ἐπὶ τὸν οἶκον Δαυείδ...πνεῦμα χάριτος. The Hebr. is 'I will pour out my Spirit'; the LXX. ἀπὸ τοῦ πνεύματός μου adds the idea of the fulness of the source; comp. Barn. i. 3 ἐκκεχυμένον ἀπὸ τοῦ πλουσίου τῆς πηγῆς Κυρίου πνεῦμα ἐφ' ὑμᾶς.

For a discussion of other points connected with the history of the Day of Pentecost I must refer to my *Credibility of the Book of the Acts*, pp. 30 ff.

[1] Ἰουδαία is here used in the large sense—the land of the Jews—which it often bears; compare, *e.g.*, Jos. *Antiq.* I. vii. 2 (εἰς τὴν τότε μὲν Χαναναίαν λεγομένην νῦν δὲ Ἰουδαίαν μετῴκηκε), Tacitus *Hist.* II. 78 (Haec [Caesarea] Judaeae caput est), Luke iv. 44, Acts x. 37.

uttermost part of the earth.' Three periods are here marked off. (i) There is the earliest period, when Jerusalem was still the home of the Christian brotherhood. (ii) There is the intermediate period, when the Church was gradually spreading over what we now call the Holy Land. Samaria is specially mentioned because the Samaritans were half Jews and half Gentiles. (iii) There is the period of world-wide extension, when the Church was evangelizing the Provinces of the Roman Empire till, having at first borne witness in Jerusalem, it at length bore witness also at Rome. Of these three periods St Luke does not give a full or exhaustive history. In each of them he selects and records typical incidents. The Confirmation scenes in the Acts are chosen, we cannot doubt, from many similar scenes. Each is a representative scene for a particular period of the Church's development. The significance of each lies in the fact that it is illustrative. The Epistles, as we shall presently see, enable us to some extent to fill in incidents of this kind which are wanting in St Luke's record.

(1) Jerusalem.

I have already spoken of the day of Pentecost. The gift of the Spirit was on that morning bestowed on representatives of the Church apart from any sacramental act or sign. The gift was divine not only in itself but in all the circumstances of its bestowal. No human ministry intervened between the Giver and the recipients. But what of the later events of that day? Were the three thousand persons confirmed who on that day received the word and were baptised? Nothing is said of any laying on of hands; and certainly we have no right to assume that to have happened which is not recorded. The occasion was wholly abnormal. But it is clear that a definite bestowal of the Holy Ghost consequent on, but distinct from, their Baptism was vouchsafed to these earliest converts to the faith. St Luke, who is characteristically brief in his narrative and is often content by a passing hint to suggest important details of the history, intimates this in his record of St Peter's exhortation and assurance (ii. 38): 'Repent ye, and be baptised every one of you in the

Name of Jesus Christ unto the remission of your sins ; and ye shall receive the gift of the Holy Ghost (καὶ λήμψεσθε τὴν δωρεὰν τοῦ ἁγίου πνεύματος).' The phrase λαβεῖν τὸ ἅγιον πνεῦμα (πνεῦμα ἅγιον) is the phrase elsewhere used by St Luke in reference to the reception of the gift of the Spirit at Confirmation (viii. 15, 17, x. 47, xix. 2 ; comp. John vii. 39, 1 Cor. ii. 12, 2 Cor. xi. 4, Gal. iii. 2, 14, Rom. viii. 15, 1 John ii. 27). For ἡ δωρεά in this connexion compare viii. 20, x. 45, xi. 17.

(2) The land of the Jews and Samaria.

In the intermediate period two typical scenes are recorded by St Luke.

(i) Samaria (viii. 12 ff.). Those who in 'the city of Samaria' believed the good news proclaimed by Philip the Evangelist 'concerning the kingdom of God and the name of Jesus Christ[1]' were baptised each one (ἐβαπτίζοντο v. 12). The Apostles at Jerusalem, hearing of the evangelization of the Samaritans, sent Peter and John as

---

[1] It is worthy of note that this twofold description of the εὐαγ-γέλιον occurs in the Acts only here and in xxviii. 23, 31, i.e. at the point where the second period of the Apostolic history begins (Samaria) and at the point where the extension of the Church to 'the uttermost part of the earth' (Rome) is related.

their representatives to this first colony of the Gospel. The two Apostles, when they came, offered prayer (clearly in the assembly of 'the Brethren') that those who had been baptised 'might receive the Holy Ghost' (ὅπως λάβωσιν πνεῦμα ἅγιον). Then the sacramental sign was conferred on each, and each 'received the Holy Ghost'— τότε ἐπετίθεσαν τὰς χεῖρας ἐπ' αὐτούς, καὶ ἐλάμβανον πνεῦμα ἅγιον. The imperfects ἐπετίθεσαν and ἐλάμβανον are pictorial; they individualize; they enable us, as it were, to see the two Apostles 'confirming' the converts one after the other and the converts one after another rejoicing in the reception of the divine gift. We note in the careful language of the historian (v. 16) the contrast between the state of those who 'had only been baptised into the name of the Lord Jesus' and the full possession of the blessings of renewal through the illapse (ἐπιπεπτωκός) of the Spirit.

(ii) Caesarea (x. 44 ff.). The typical Confirmation scene just noticed is laid at 'the city of Samaria.' The next is laid at Caesarea, the capital of Judaea, the country of the Jews (comp. Tacitus quoted above, p. 22 *n*). St Peter was prepared by a vision for the invitation of the Roman Centurion. When the Apostle reached Caesarea, he was met by Cornelius and entered into his house. While he was speaking to him and the 'many' that were 'come together,' 'the Holy Ghost fell on all those who were hearing the word.' No scruple, the Apostle urged, could be felt by any as to the baptism of those whom God had thus accepted. At his command they were 'baptised in the name of Jesus Christ.' In the case of this assembly of Gentiles, as in the case of the Apostles themselves, there was no sacramental act or sign. The Holy Ghost was given independently of any 'laying on of hands.' The fact marks the occasion as the Gentile Pentecost (xi. 15 ὥσπερ καὶ ἐφ' ἡμᾶς ἐν ἀρχῇ). The historian in this narrative, as in the record of the Day of Pentecost (ii. 17, 33), is careful to use the Pentecostal keyword which he employs nowhere else—ἐπὶ τὰ ἔθνη ἡ δωρεὰ τοῦ πνεύματος τοῦ ἁγίου ἐκκέχυται (*v.* 45). Here was a typical fulfilment of the promise that 'in the last days' God

would 'pour forth of his Spirit upon all
flesh' (ii. 17, Joel ii. 28). Hence the
emphasis laid on this outpouring of the
Spirit in the immediate sequel (xi. 15 ff.),
when St Peter at Jerusalem defended his
action, and later in the same Apostle's
speech (xv. 8) at the Council of Jerusalem,
when the liberty of the Gentile Churches
had to be vindicated. This history, let us
remark, is a warning against two opposite
and very common temptations—(i) the
temptation to undervalue the sacraments;
even after the converts had received the
gift of the Spirit, the Apostle gave command
that they should be baptised; (ii) the
temptation to deny or to endeavour to
explain away manifestations of divine grace
in those who have had no part in outward
ordinances. This latter point is of special
importance in regard to the subject under
discussion. A clear and strong conviction
of the blessing of Confirmation does not
justify us in remaining blind to the signs
of the presence of the Spirit in the holy
men and women who have had no part in,
or who even reject, the rite of Confirmation.
He who is most loyal to the order of the

Catholic Church will rejoice in every token that the bounty of the Father in Heaven is not limited by that order.

One other incident belonging to this period demands notice. The Acts contains two accounts of the visit of Ananias to Saul of Tarsus after his conversion (ix. 10 ff., xxii. 12 ff.). In both the historian tells us of the Baptism of Saul. In the earlier of the two passages he speaks also of a 'laying on of hands.' Ananias in a vision receives a divine command to go to Saul; for Saul too has had a vision and has seen Ananias 'coming in and laying his hands on him, that he might receive his sight.' Ananias obeys. He goes to Saul and, laying his hands on him, says 'Brother Saul, the Lord, even Jesus, who appeared unto thee in the way which thou camest, hath sent me, that thou mayest receive thy sight and be filled with the Holy Ghost.' 'And straightway,' St Luke adds, 'there fell from his eyes as it were scales, and he received his sight; and he arose and was baptised.' It can hardly be questioned by those who, in view of the reinforcement of tradition by the internal evidence of the Book itself, regard St Luke as the author of the Acts, that St Luke derived his information as to the conversion of St Paul from the Apostle himself. We have good reason therefore for believing that the compressed narrative of the visit of Ananias to Saul of Tarsus gives with approximate accuracy the words spoken by Ananias and the true sequence of events. We learn then that a 'disciple,' who apparently held no official position in the Church, received a divine commission to admit Saul of Tarsus, the persecutor, into the Church of the redeemed; that so divinely commissioned he laid his hands on him, conferring thereby on him a twofold gift, the gift of physical restoration and the gift of the Holy Spirit; and that immediately afterwards Saul was baptised. The restoration of sight was doubtless to Saul a pledge of the reality of the spiritual endowment (comp. Mark ii. 6 ff., Matt. ix. 3 ff., Luke v. 21 ff.). Here, as in the case of Cornelius and his friends, the gift of the Spirit preceded Baptism. If we hesitate to regard Ananias' 'laying on of hands' as a conscious and formal act of Confirmation, yet at any rate the history witnesses to the habitual recognition in the Apostolic Church of a close connexion between 'the laying on of hands' and the bestowal of the Holy Spirit.

(3) The extension of the Church to 'the uttermost part of the earth.'

In the period of world-wide extension St Luke selects one Confirmation scene. Ephesus was the great centre of Asiatic idolatry, a typical stronghold of false worship. When St Paul arrived there (xix. 1 ff.) and found 'certain disciples,' he is represented as asking them the question 'Did ye receive the Holy Ghost when ye believed? (εἰ πνεῦμα ἅγιον ἐλάβετε πιστεύσαντες;).' The question does not look to an inner consciousness which the 'disciples' might have had of the presence and influence of the Holy Spirit but to a definite reception of the Holy Spirit at the beginning of their Christian life (πιστεύσαντες) of such a kind that, if it had been vouchsafed to them, they could not but remember it. The Apostle assumed that, if they were 'disciples,' they must have been baptised. He is anxious to know if their Baptism had been followed by their Confirmation. When they answered that they had indeed been baptised, but baptised only with John's Baptism, he explained to them the Baptist's work and faith in Jesus. 'And when they heard this, they were baptised into the name of the Lord Jesus. And when Paul had laid his hands upon them, the Holy Ghost came on them.' The question of St Paul is very significant. There is nothing in the narrative to lead us to suppose that he followed at Ephesus a course which he did not follow elsewhere. It was natural to him to ascertain whether such converts as he found in this place or in that had received the grace of Confirmation. It is equally clear from the history that it was his regular practice to confirm by the laying on of hands those who had been baptised. Further, the question reveals what was commonly but not universally the case in the Apostolic age with those who had been baptised. It was to be hoped, but it was not to be assumed, that they had 'received the Holy Ghost.' If they had not, the explanation might lie in the fact that they owed their conversion to an evangelist who had authority to baptise but not to confirm (comp. viii. 12, 14 ff.).

A review of these historical notices, which, it will be remembered, are representative, brings out the following points: (1) In the Apostolic Church a definite bestowal of the Holy Spirit normally followed Baptism[1]. (2) The outward and visible sign was the 'laying on of hands.' (3) The gift was sometimes evidenced by an extraordinary 'manifestation of the Spirit,' tongues (ii. 4, x. 46, xix. 6) and prophecy (xix. 6). But this was not always so. In the case of the converts at Samaria (viii. 17) and, we may add, of Saul of Tarsus (ix. 17 f.), no such 'manifestation' is recorded. Such an extraordinary 'manifestation' then, whatever its varying forms[2], was not of the essence of the gift but was rather an accidental result of the Spirit's presence. St Paul mentions 'prophecy' and 'divers kinds of tongues' among many

---

[1] This was not the case, so far as the record goes, in the following instances, (1) the Baptism of the Ethiopian Eunuch by Philip the Evangelist (viii. 38) ; (2) of Lydia and her house at Philippi (xvi. 15); (3) of the jailor at Philippi (xvi. 33) ; (4) of the converts at Corinth (xviii. 8).

[2] For a discussion as to the nature of 'tongues' I must refer to my *Credibility of the Book of the Acts*, pp. 35 ff.

other modes of the 'manifestation of the Spirit' (1 Cor. xii. 4 ff., 28 ff.); and he clearly does not rank 'tongues' as among the highest of the Spirit's gifts (1 Cor. xiii., xiv.). (4) The minister, at least normally, was an Apostle. (5) 'Laying on of hands' was not confined to one school of the Apostles. The rite was administered by the Apostles of the Circumcision and by the Apostle of the Gentiles. The imposition of hands after Baptism is represented as the natural act of the Apostles in the case of their converts. No explanation of the origin of the practice is given. In the first days it had a place in the life of the Church. Short of an express statement to that effect we could have no more convincing proof that herein the Apostles were following a command which they had received from the Lord Himself.

II. *Passages of the Apostolic Epistles which speak of an outward and visible sign in Confirmation and of the corresponding inward and spiritual grace.*

2 Timothy i. 6 f. δι' ἣν αἰτίαν ἀναμιμνήσκω σε ἀναζωπυρεῖν τὸ χάρισμα τοῦ θεοῦ, ὅ ἐστιν ἐν σοὶ διὰ τῆς ἐπιθέσεως τῶν χειρῶν μου· οὐ γὰρ ἔδωκεν ἡμῖν ὁ θεὸς πνεῦμα δειλίας, ἀλλὰ δυνάμεως καὶ ἀγάπης καὶ σωφρονισμοῦ.

It is perhaps universally assumed that these words refer to Timothy's Ordination: so Chrysostom, τουτέστι, τὴν χάριν τοῦ πνεύματος, ἣν ἔλαβες εἰς προστασίαν τῆς ἐκκλησίας, εἰς σημεῖα, εἰς τὴν λατρείαν ἅπασαν. But the oftener I read the passage, the clearer, I confess, it seems to me that St Paul has in view not Timothy's Ordination but Timothy's Confirmation. For this opinion I will give my reasons.

It is convenient to turn first to that passage in the First Epistle (1 Tim. iv. 14) which is commonly regarded as referring to the same occasion as our present passage. The words are these: μὴ ἀμέλει

τοῦ ἐν σοὶ χαρίσματος, ὃ ἐδόθη σοι διὰ
προφητείας μετὰ ἐπιθέσεως τῶν χειρῶν τοῦ
πρεσβυτερίου. The fact that in one
passage the allusion is to the 'laying on of
the hands of the presbytery' and in the
other to the 'laying on of my hands' does
not in itself seem to me a serious difficulty
in the way of supposing that the two
passages have the same event in view.
An Apostle, as a Bishop now, would
doubtless take the leading place among the
presbyters in an act of Ordination; and in
the fervour of a personal appeal he might
well refer exclusively to his own part in
the solemn rite of blessing. Yet the
impression produced by the difference of
language is that the two passages allude to
two different occasions. And this impression is greatly strengthened when we
examine the context of the two passages.
In the verses which precede the earlier
passage (1 Tim. iv. 11 ff.) Timothy is
regarded as a leader. He is to 'command
and teach,' to shew himself a 'pattern to
the faithful,' to 'give attention' to the
public reading of Scripture, to public
exhortation, and to public teaching. It is

that he may fulfil these duties of a pastor and teacher that he is to be careful not to 'neglect the gift that is in him.' The context in the later passage is wholly different. St Paul recalls 'the unfeigned faith' which was 'in' Timothy, a faith, he adds, which 'dwelt first in thy grandmother Lois and thy mother Eunice.' The assurance that in Christian faith Timothy resembled his Mother and his Grandmother is the occasion of the appeal which follows: 'For the which cause I put thee in remembrance that thou ever kindle into flame the gift of God, which is in thee through the laying on of my hands.' There is nothing here which leads up to the thought of the grace of Ordination. The mention of Timothy's Mother and Grandmother suggests that the *charisma* which Timothy is ever to keep alive is one which is bestowed on all faithful people, and that the occasion when he received the 'outward and visible sign' of its bestowal was at an early stage of his Christian life. Again, how is the *charisma* described? 'For God gave us not a spirit of fearfulness (δειλίας), but of power and love and soberness (σωφρονισμοῦ).'

When St Paul speaks of 'us,' does he
mean 'us disciples' or 'us to whom a
ministry or an oversight has been com-
mitted'? I do not doubt that he here
regards himself and Timothy simply as
members of the Church. For the negative
clause, 'not a spirit of fearfulness,' recalls
at once the wide and general language of
an earlier Epistle, 'Ye received not the
spirit of bondage again unto fear, but ye
received the spirit of adoption' (Rom. viii.
15; comp. Gal. iv. 6); and the gifts of
'power' and 'love' and 'soberness' are
catholic gifts, gifts, that is, which are
common to all those who are 'in Christ
Jesus.'[1] Lastly, we turn to the succeeding
context. The inference of duty ($o\hat{v}\nu$)
which the Apostle draws for Timothy from
the premiss of assured endowment is that
he must not be 'ashamed of the testimony
of our Lord nor of me his prisoner'
(comp. *v.* 16); he must 'suffer hardship
with the gospel[2] according to the power

---

[1] For δύναμις compare *e.g.* Eph. iii. 16, Col. i. 11; for ἀγάπη
e.g. 1 Cor. xii. 31—xiv. 1; for σωφρονισμός *e.g.* Rom. xii. 3, 1 Tim.
ii. 9, 15, Titus ii. 2, 5 f., 12.
[2] Comp. Phil. i. 27 f. συναθλοῦντες τῇ πίστει τοῦ εὐαγγελίου
καὶ μὴ πτυρόμενοι κ.τ.λ.

of God, who saved us and called us with an holy calling.' Here too the 'us' is certainly 'us Christians.' The 'holy calling' (comp. 2 Thess. i. 11, 1 Cor. i. 26, Phil. iii. 14, Eph. iv. 1, 4) looks back to the first beginning of the Christian life. The duties to which St Paul summons Timothy are such as are binding on all the people of God. A review of the whole passage then leads to the conclusion that St Paul, conscious that he is now nearing his end, recalls to Timothy's mind an occasion, which both of them would vividly remember, when, his 'beloved child' (1 Cor. iv. 17) having been 'baptised into the name of the Lord Jesus,' he himself 'laid his hands on him and the Holy Ghost came upon him' (comp. Acts xix. 6). It is not difficult to find a place for this occasion in the history recorded in the Acts. When during his second missionary journey St Paul revisited Lystra, Timothy was already a 'disciple' and already well known to the 'brethren' both at Lystra and at Iconium (Acts xvi. 2). Clearly he was not now a 'neophyte.' We are precluded then from connecting his Confirmation with this visit of St Paul to Timothy's home. It must have taken place during St Paul's earlier sojourn at Lystra (Acts xiv. 8 ff.). The narrative of the Apostle's first visit to Lystra is wholly occupied with the healing of the cripple and its sequel. But it contains an incidental reference to successful evangelistic work. When the Jews who came from Antioch and Iconium had stoned St Paul and dragging him out of the city had left him, ' the disciples,' it is said, stood round his seemingly dead body. St Paul then did not leave Lystra till he had planted an infant Church there. Of the disciples who were ' the first fruit' of Lycaonia it is no extravagant conjecture that Timothy was one. During this first visit to Lystra Timothy, we may reasonably suppose, was baptised and had the Apostle's hands laid on him. The Epistle then supplements the story of the Acts. To the one Confirmation scene of St Paul's ministry recorded in the Acts it adds another and an earlier Confirmation scene. It strengthens the inference which we drew from the account of what took place at Ephesus, that the Apostle was wont, after his converts had been baptised, to lay his hands on them that they might receive the endowment of the Spirit. Further, it is to be especially noticed that the grace of Confirmation in the Epistle does not lie in any extraordinary 'manifestation of the Spirit,' such as tongues or prophecy or the working of miracles, but in the bestowal of a purely spiritual endowment, 'power and love and soberness.'

Hebrews vi. 1 f. ἐπὶ τὴν τελειότητα φερώμεθα, μὴ πάλιν θεμέλιον καταβαλλόμενοι μετανοίας ἀπὸ νεκρῶν ἔργων, καὶ πίστεως ἐπὶ θεόν, βαπτισμῶν διδαχῆς (v. l. διδαχὴν) ἐπιθέσεώς τε χειρῶν, ἀναστάσεως (v. l. ἀναστάσεώς τε) νεκρῶν καὶ κρίματος αἰωνίου.

A few words must first be said as to the closely related subjects of reading and of construction in the clause with which we are immediately concerned (βαπτισμῶν... χειρῶν). The reading διδαχῆς is found in ℵACDvg; διδαχήν in Bd. The former reading, being that found in different groups of MSS. representing different types of text, must, I think, be regarded as the better supported reading. Codex B is

undoubtedly a high authority; but to accept
a reading practically supported by it alone
seems to attribute to it undue weight,
unless indeed such a reading commends
itself strongly on the ground of intrinsic
probability.   The reverse of this appears
to be the case here.   If we take the reading
διδαχήν, it is in apposition to θεμέλιον, on
which depend the genitives μετανοίας and
πίστεως.   When the regimen of θεμέλιον
has once been broken by διδαχήν, it is
impossible to revert to θεμέλιον in regard
to the genitives of the final clause ἀναστάσεως and κρίματος.   These two latter
genitives must in that case depend on
διδαχήν.   The adoption then of the reading
διδαχήν (1) dislocates the passage, cutting
off two of the three clauses from connexion
with the essential idea conveyed in the
word θεμέλιον; (2) it fails to recognise the
difference between the abstract terms
'repentance,' 'faith,' 'resurrection,' 'judgment' and on the other hand the terms
describing the definite and concrete acts of
'baptism' and 'laying on of hands.'   The
addition of the word 'teaching' in reference
to these latter words is necessary in order

to correlate them with the other four
words. Hence, though Westcott and Hort
prefer διδαχήν, I venture on the ground
both of documentary evidence and of internal considerations to adopt the reading
διδαχῆς. The word διδαχῆς denotes the
'inward and spiritual' meaning of the two
'outward and visible signs,' βαπτισμοί and
ἐπίθεσις χειρῶν.

We next enquire what is the reference
in βαπτισμῶν and ἐπιθέσεως χειρῶν. Bishop
Westcott *in loco* maintains that the former
term includes 'Christian Baptism and other
lustral rites,' adding that 'the teaching
would naturally be directed to shew their
essential difference.' He gives a somewhat
similarly inclusive meaning to the 'laying
on of hands,' regarding it as 'the expressive
symbol of a solemn blessing (Matt. xix. 13),
of the restoration or communication of
strength for a definite work.' Such too in
general is the interpretation of the former
term given by Dr Vaughan in his com-
mentary on the Epistle; though he explains
the latter as 'that *sequel and complement of
baptism* of which we have examples in
Acts viii. 17 and xix. 6.' No one can

lightly differ from these two masters of
exegesis. Yet I confess that I cannot
accept their interpretation. For (1) the
writer of the Epistle disparages such
'lustral rites' as being δικαιώματα σαρκὸς
μέχρι καιροῦ διορθώσεως ἐπικείμενα (ix. 10);
it cannot be part of the 'foundation' to
shew the insufficiency of these; the
'teaching' which is part of the 'foundation'
must be positive, not controversial; (2) the
reference to 'repentance' and 'faith' leads
on to the mention not of 'lustral rites'
generally but of Christian Baptism speci-
fically (comp. Acts ii. 38); (3) the writer
marks the great crises of the Christian life
here and hereafter; the Christian man
'repents' and 'believes'; he is 'baptised'
and 'confirmed'; he will 'rise' and be
'judged.' Another interpretation of the
plural βαπτισμῶν then must be sought.
Now just as e.g. ἀσπασμός means an act
of salutation, so βαπτισμός (ix. 10, Mark
vii. 4, Col. ii. 12 v. l.) means an act of
baptism or washing. The phrase διδαχὴ
βαπτισμῶν therefore signifies 'the teaching
about acts of washing,' the exposition of
the truths and spiritual principles embodied

44

and expressed in the baptism of this disciple and of that. The exact expression seems chosen to denote not the Christian rite in the abstract ($βάπτισμα$) but the Christian rite in its concrete application to individual believers (comp. x. 22). If this interpretation of $βαπτισμῶν$ is correct, the meaning of $ἐπιθέσεως χειρῶν$ is fixed. It cannot be general and inclusive; it must exclusively denote that act of spiritual blessing which in the Apostolic Church normally followed Baptism.

The question still remains What was the writer's conception of the 'teaching' to which he refers? The answer is given in three passages of the Epistle, one of these being in the immediate context of the passage which we have just been considering.

(a) vi. 4 $τοὺς$ $ἅπαξ$ $φωτισθέντας$, $γευσαμένους$ $τε$ $τῆς$ $δωρεᾶς$ $τῆς$ $ἐπουρανίου$ $καὶ$ $μετόχους$ $γενηθέντας$ $πνεύματος$ $ἁγίου$, $καὶ$ $καλὸν$ $γευσαμένους$ $θεοῦ$ $ῥῆμα$ $κ.τ.λ$. The writer is describing persons whom 'it is impossible to renew again unto repentance.' They are those who 'were once for all enlightened and tasted in its beauty the word of God and the powers of the world to come and fell away.' He further defines what he meant by the words 'who were once for all enlightened   They were 'enlightened' 'in that (*or* when) they both tasted the heavenly gift and became partakers of the Holy Ghost.' The φωτισμός has two parts (τε...καί). First those who were 'enlightened' consciously realized their part in God's gift of the 'only begotten Son' (John iii. 16; comp. Rom. v. 15, 17) and in God's gifts that are 'in Christ,' the gift of 'eternal life' (1 John v. 11) and the gift of sonship (John i. 12). This manifold gift of redemption and renewal is pledged to all who are 'baptised into Jesus Christ' (Gal. iii. 27, Rom. vi. 3). The allusion then in these words is to Baptism. Secondly those who were 'enlightened' had a participation in the endowment of Pentecost; 'they became partakers of the Holy Ghost.' This participation in the Holy Ghost was, as we learn from the Acts, conveyed to believers by the 'laying on of hands.' In these words therefore the writer clearly defines the 'teaching about baptisms and the laying on of hands' of which he has just spoken.

(*b*) ii. 3 f. ἥτις [sc. σωτηρία], ἀρχὴν λαβοῦσα λαλεῖσθαι διὰ τοῦ κυρίου, ὑπὸ τῶν ἀκουσάντων εἰς ἡμᾶς ἐβεβαιώθη, συνεπιμαρτυροῦντος τοῦ θεοῦ...πνεύματος ἁγίου μερισμοῖς κατὰ τὴν ἑαυτοῦ θέλησιν. The mind of the writer goes back to the time when the message of salvation was first brought to him and to his friends (εἰς ἡμᾶς) by evangelists who had themselves heard the Lord, and when God bore His witness to the message of the Gospel by a bestowal of the Spirit as definite and unmistakeable as 'the signs and wonders' to which he refers. The passage recalls some Confirmation scene or scenes in some Palestinian Church such as the representative Confirmation scene which St Luke records as taking place in 'the city of Samaria' (Acts viii. 14 ff.). It is a strong and circumstantial testimony to the truth of the narratives contained in the Acts.

(*c*) x. 29 ὁ τὸν υἱὸν τοῦ θεοῦ καταπατήσας, καὶ τὸ αἷμα τῆς διαθήκης κοινὸν ἡγησάμενος ἐν ᾧ ἡγιάσθη, καὶ τὸ πνεῦμα τῆς χάριτος ἐνυβρίσας. 'The language used,' writes Bishop Westcott *in loco*, 'suggests the open repudiation of the baptismal confession and covenant.' That the writer has in view the initiation of the Christian life appears from the words ἐν ᾧ ἡγιάσθη (comp. 1 Cor. vi. 11). In his baptism the man was 'sanctified' 'in the blood of the covenant.' Having been 'baptised into Jesus Christ' he rejects Christ—note the august title 'the Son of God'; comp. vi. 6—and His redemption. In another passage of the Epistle (x. 22) the 'outward and visible sign' is made prominent, λελουσμένοι τὸ σῶμα ὕδατι καθαρῷ: here 'the inward and spiritual grace.' In the words which follow—'hath done despite unto the Spirit of grace'—the allusion to the gift in Confirmation is no less clear. The special phrase, 'the Spirit of grace,' is significant. The Spirit given in Confirmation is the vehicle to those who are 'in Christ' of 'the manifold grace of God' (1 Pet. iv. 10).

Thus the writer of the Epistle reveals incidentally what is his conception of that 'teaching about baptisms and the laying on of hands' which he reckons as pertaining to the 'foundation.' In Baptism the convert realizes his own part in God's gift of Christ and of the blessings involved in that supreme gift. As his 'body is washed with pure water,' so he is 'sanctified in' the blood of Christ. In Confirmation he is made a 'partaker of the Holy Ghost,' in whom the divine grace is embodied and bestowed. Together Baptism and Confirmation are an 'enlightenment.' Henceforth, if he is faithful, he can 'walk in the light,' 'the true light' which 'now shineth' (1 John i. 7, ii. 8).

We can now estimate the significance of the passage of the Epistle (vi. 1 f.) from which we started. (i) We learn the close association in the Apostolic age of Baptism and Confirmation. Through them the convert was brought into personal relation with the great gifts of God bestowed on man in the Incarnation and in Pentecost. (ii) We learn the name of Confirmation current in the Apostolic age—ἐπίθεσις χειρῶν, 'the laying on of hands.' (iii) We learn the importance which in the Apostolic age was attached to these two sacramental acts and their spiritual meaning. (iv) We learn that the gift of the Spirit in the

Apostolic age was not essentially connected with any so called miraculous powers. (v) We learn that in the Apostolic age Confirmation as well as Baptism was the acknowledged inheritance of Christians of different schools of thought. The unknown writer of the Epistle to the Hebrews was a Jew; but the tone and temper of his teaching was not that of St Paul or of the Apostles of the Circumcision. He was deeply embued with the literary culture and the philosophic thought of Alexandria. His Epistle shews us that, however widely the first disciples differed in their interpretation of some elements of Christian truth, there was no divergence of practice or of thought in regard to Baptism and Confirmation.

We have now reviewed all the passages in the New Testament which speak of the laying on of hands in connexion with Confirmation. Is there any indirect allusion to this outward and visible sign in the Apostolic writings? I cannot but think that such an allusion is to be found in the three passages in which St Paul speaks of a divine sealing. They are these :

2 Corinthians i. 21 f. ὁ δὲ βεβαιῶν ἡμᾶς σὺν ὑμῖν εἰς Χριστὸν καὶ χρίσας ἡμᾶς θεός, ὁ καὶ σφραγισάμενος ἡμᾶς καὶ δοὺς τὸν ἀρραβῶνα τοῦ πνεύματος ἐν ταῖς καρδίαις ἡμῶν.

Ephesians i. 13 f. ἐν ᾧ [sc. τῷ χριστῷ] καὶ ὑμεῖς ἀκούσαντες τὸν λόγον τῆς ἀληθείας, τὸ εὐαγγέλιον τῆς σωτηρίας ὑμῶν, ἐν ᾧ καὶ πιστεύσαντες, ἐσφραγίσθητε τῷ πνεύματι τῆς ἐπαγγελίας τῷ ἁγίῳ, ὅ [v. l. ὅς] ἐστιν ἀρραβὼν τῆς κληρονομίας ἡμῶν, εἰς ἀπολύτρωσιν τῆς περιποιήσεως, εἰς ἔπαινον τῆς δόξης αὐτοῦ.

Ephesians iv. 30 καὶ μὴ λυπεῖτε τὸ πνεῦμα τὸ ἅγιον τοῦ θεοῦ, ἐν ᾧ ἐσφραγίσθητε εἰς ἡμέραν ἀπολυτρώσεως.

In each of these passages the sealing is intimately connected with the gift of the Holy Spirit. The Holy Spirit is the χαρακτήρ, the 'impress' or 'stamp' which is imparted and which abides. He who 'seals' is God. We have a close parallel to these passages in John vi. 27 τοῦτον γὰρ ὁ πατὴρ ἐσφράγισεν ὁ θεός: the Father 'sealed' the Incarnate Son by the Spirit

who abode on Him (John i. 32, iii. 34).
Further, in these passages the use of the
aorist shews that the reference is to a
definite crisis of the Christian life in the
past. In 2 Cor. i. 21 f. the present parti-
ciple ($\beta \epsilon \beta \alpha \iota \hat{\omega} \nu$) gives place to a series of
aorist participles ($\chi \rho i \sigma \alpha s$, $\sigma \phi \rho \alpha \gamma \iota \sigma \acute{\alpha} \mu \epsilon \nu o s$,
$\delta o \acute{\upsilon} s$). In Eph. i. 13 f. it is clear that the
allusion is to the time when the converts
became believers ($\dot{\alpha} \kappa o \acute{\upsilon} \sigma \alpha \nu \tau \epsilon s \ldots \pi \iota \sigma \tau \epsilon \acute{\upsilon} \sigma \alpha \nu$-
$\tau \epsilon s \ \dot{\epsilon} \sigma \phi \rho \alpha \gamma \acute{\iota} \sigma \theta \eta \tau \epsilon$); compare Acts xix. 2 $\epsilon \dot{\iota}$
$\pi \nu \epsilon \hat{\upsilon} \mu \alpha \ \ddot{\alpha} \gamma \iota o \nu \ \dot{\epsilon} \lambda \acute{\alpha} \beta \epsilon \tau \epsilon \ \pi \iota \sigma \tau \epsilon \acute{\upsilon} \sigma \alpha \nu \tau \epsilon s$; There
can be no doubt then that St Paul in these
passages has in mind the bestowal of the
Holy Spirit in Confirmation. Now the
metaphor of sealing suggests not only the
ideas of possession and of consequent
security but also that of a certain character
being impressed on the person who is
sealed. This latter idea is vividly and, so
to speak, pictorially expressed by 'the
laying on of hands.' Just as the washing
of the neophyte in Baptism is the outward
and visible sign that God cleanses him from
his sins, so the imposition of hands with
prayer for the Holy Spirit is the outward
and visible sign that God seals him with

the Holy Spirit. The divine sealing is the heavenly and spiritual counterpart of the human and earthly act of the laying on of hands. When St Paul speaks of God sealing men with the Holy Spirit, he seems to be indirectly alluding to the ministers of Christ laying their hands on the converts and praying for them that they might receive the Holy Ghost (Acts viii. 15).

But at this point another question suggests itself. In the Apostolic Church was the laying on of hands the only outward and visible sign used in Confirmation? Or was unction also a recognised symbol? Three lines of argument converge to suggest an affirmative answer to the latter question.

(1) Laying on of hands and anointing are in the Bible closely related symbolical acts. According to Numbers viii. 10 the Levites were originally set apart by a laying on of hands: 'the children of Israel shall lay their hands upon the Levites.' The Priests and in particular

the High Priest were anointed (*e.g.* Ex. xxviii. 41). In New Testament times both actions were used in regard to the sick. Both the Lord Himself and the Apostles laid their hands on the sick (*e.g.* Mark vi. 5, viii. 23, Acts xxviii. 8). The Apostles when our Lord first sent them forth in Galilee anointed the sick (Mark vi. 13); and St James, writing 'to the twelve tribes which are of the Dispersion,' enjoins (v. 14) that prayers should be offered for the recovery of the sick accompanied by anointing. It would be very natural therefore if in Confirmation both laying on of hands and unction were employed by the Apostles and their followers.

(2) In the sub-apostolic literature there is, so far as I know, no clear allusion to Confirmation. But in the writings of Tertullian, which belong to the end of the second century and to the beginning of the third, Confirmation holds an assured place in the sacramental system of the Church. The language used by this Father implies that he is referring to established customs in his own Church of Carthage; and among these customs was an anointing of the

baptised immediately preceding the laying
on of hands. The chief passages are these:

de Baptismo vii., viii. Exinde egressi
de lavacro perungimur benedicta unctione
de pristina disciplina, qua ungi oleo de
cornu in sacerdotio solebant......Dehinc
manus imponitur, per benedictionem advo-
cans et invitans Spiritum Sanctum.

de Resurrectione Carnis viii. Scilicet
caro abluitur ut anima emaculetur: caro
ungitur ut anima consecretur: caro signatur[1]
ut et anima muniatur: caro manus impositione adumbratur ut et anima spiritu
illuminetur: caro corpore et sanguine Christi
vescitur ut et anima de Deo saginetur.

A fuller description of this rite is given
in the Canons of Hippolytus (ed. Achelis
p. 98): ' Ubi ex aqua ascendit, presbyter
prehendit chrisma εὐχαριστίας et signat
frontem et os et pectus ejus signo crucis
ungitque totum corpus ejus et caput et
faciem dicens: Ego te ungo in nomine Patris
et Filii et Spiritus Sancti...Ibi episcopus
manum imponens omnibus qui baptizati

---

[1] The allusion is to the signing with the sign of the cross;
comp. *e.g. ad Uxorem* ii. 5 (Latebisne tu, cum lectulum, cum
corpusculum tuum signas?), 8 (furtiva signatio).

sunt, haec orat dicens: Benedicimus tibi,
omnipotens Domine Deus, quia hos dignos
reddidisti, qui iterum nascerentur, et super
quos Spiritum Tuum Sanctum effundis, ut
jam uniti sint corpori ecclesiae.' If, as
seems probable, these Canons are substantially those of Hippolytus and this
portion of them original, we have evidence
that at Rome about 230 A.D. unction was
practised as a rite preparatory to the laying
on of hands.

Irenaeus enables us to carry the evidence somewhat further back. In the first
of his five Books against Heresies[1] (ed.
Massuet) i. 21. 3 he tells us that a certain
Gnostic sect, the Marcosians, anointed the
person who had just been baptised—ἔπειτα
μυρίζουσι τὸν τετελεσμένον τῷ ὀπῷ τῷ ἀπὸ
βαλσάμου· τὸ γὰρ μύρον τοῦτο τύπον τῆς
ὑπὲρ τὰ ὅλα εὐωδίας εἶναι λέγουσιν. There
can be little doubt that the rites and liturgical formulae of the Gnostic sects were
derived from, and were a parody of, the
rites and liturgical formulae of the Catholic

---

[1] The third book was written during the episcopate of
Eleutherus (iii. 3. 3). Eleutherus was Bishop of Rome A.D. 175—
190.

Church. We infer therefore that this unction was a custom in the Church when the Marcosians broke away from it, and that consequently it must have been in use at least as early as the middle of the second century.

It seems however very improbable that, while unction had an acknowledged place as a religious rite in the Old Testament and was practised at least to some extent in Apostolic times together with laying on of hands in the healing of the sick, it should have sprung up independently in the Church of the second century in close connexion with the laying on of hands in Confirmation. It is far more probable that the unction of which, for example, Tertullian speaks was a survival from Apostolic days.

(3) We now turn to two passages of the New Testament, viz., 2 Cor. i. 21 f., 1 John ii. 20, 27.

2 Corinthians i. 21 f. (quoted above p. 51). Here a divine act of anointing is spoken of side by side with a divine act of sealing, and both are intimately connected with the gift of the Spirit. We saw that in all probability this sealing is to be regarded as

the heavenly counterpart of the earthly sign of laying on of hands. In the same way is it not natural to look upon the divine anointing as the spiritual reality figured by an anointing with material oil?

1 John ii. 20, 27 καὶ ὑμεῖς χρίσμα ἔχετε ἀπὸ τοῦ ἁγίου· οἴδατε πάντες—οὐκ ἔγραψα (v. l. καὶ οἴδατε πάντα. οὐκ ἔγραψα) ὑμῖν ὅτι οὐκ οἴδατε τὴν ἀλήθειαν, ἀλλ᾽ ὅτι οἴδατε αὐτήν, καὶ ὅτι πᾶν ψεῦδος ἐκ τῆς ἀληθείας οὐκ ἔστιν...καὶ ὑμεῖς τὸ χρίσμα ὃ ἐλάβετε ἀπ᾽ αὐτοῦ μένει ἐν ὑμῖν, καὶ οὐ χρείαν ἔχετε ἵνα τις διδάσκῃ ὑμᾶς· ἀλλ᾽ ὡς τὸ αὐτοῦ χρίσμα διδάσκει ὑμᾶς περὶ πάντων, καὶ ἀληθές ἐστιν καὶ οὐκ ἔστιν ψεῦδος, καὶ καθὼς ἐδίδαξεν ὑμᾶς, μένετε ἐν αὐτῷ.

St John is here speaking of the 'many anti-christs' who had arisen. Against their deceits Christians are fore-armed. They all have a teacher in the unction which they received. It abides in them. It teaches them 'concerning all things.' They 'know the truth.' What then is this unction, this anointing oil? A comparison of St John's language in the Gospel (xiv. 16, 26, xvi. 13) with his language here leaves us in no doubt. What is there said of the Holy

Spirit is here said of the unction. The unction of the Epistle is the Spirit. The unction, the Spirit, had been bestowed on the Christians to whom St John wrote at a definite time to which they could look back (ὃ ἐλάβετε v. 27; comp. Acts xix. 2). I cannot doubt that the Apostle recalls to the minds of his friends the pledge which they received in their Confirmation. But if so, is the term 'unction' wholly metaphorical (comp. Luke iv. 18, Acts iv. 27, x. 38)? The allusion to the unction is to us abrupt and startling. Nothing in the passage has prepared the way for it. No explanation is given. It seems to require some context of personal sacred association. It can hardly be questioned that the whole passage gains in force, directness, and intelligibility, if we assume that unction was used among those to whom St John wrote as a symbol of the bestowal of the Holy Spirit in Confirmation.

When then we weigh all these considerations, it becomes exceedingly probable that in Apostolic times besides the laying on of hands anointing was used as an outward and visible sign in the rite of

Confirmation. Such a supposition at once explains the language of St Paul and of St John and accounts for the custom of later times. But it must be carefully noted that we have no explicit evidence as to Apostolic usage and that our conclusion is no more than a probable inference. The Church of England as a national branch of the Catholic Church is fully justified in dispensing with a symbol which, as the evidence when carefully considered seems clearly to shew, was not universal in the Apostolic Churches and in retaining only the laying on of hands. This undoubtedly was the regular Apostolic sign in Confirmation; it is in itself simpler and is more in harmony with Western and modern customs and ideas.

At this point it will be well to endeavour to ascertain the meaning of these two symbolical acts, (1) the laying on of hands and (2) anointing. In all such enquiries it must be remembered that symbolism belongs to the poetry of life and is not

capable of a precise and rigid explanation. It must be enough if we ask
ourselves what are the main ideas which
find natural expression in any symbolical
act, and what are the associations which
have gathered round it. The following is
an attempt to classify the uses of these two
symbolical actions in the Old and in the
New Testament.

I. *The laying on of hands.*

Old Testament.

1. In blessing :

Gen. xlviii. 14 ff. (Jacob blessing
Ephraim and Manasseh).

2. In appointment to a work or office:

(i) Numb. viii. 10 f. ('The children
of Israel shall lay their hands upon the
Levites : and Aaron shall offer the Levites
before the Lord for a wave offering, on the
behalf of the children of Israel, that they
may be to do the service of the Lord').

(ii) Numb. xxvii. 18 ff. ('And the Lord

said unto Moses, Take thee Joshua the son of Nun, a man in whom is the spirit, and *lay thine hand upon him...And thou shalt put of thine honour upon him*, that all the congregation of the children of Israel may obey'). Deut. xxxiv. 9 ('And Joshua the son of Nun was *full of the spirit of wisdom; for Moses had laid his hands upon him*').

3. In the ritual of sacrifices:

Ex. xxix. 10, 15, 19, Lev. i. 4, 10 (LXX), iii. 2, 8, 13, iv. 4, 24, 29, 33, viii. 14, 18, xvi. 21, 2 Chron. xxix. 23. All these passages except the last are from the Priest's Code. The most important passage—it is interpretative—is Lev. xvi. 21 f., 'And Aaron shall lay both his hands upon the head of the live goat, and confess over him all the iniquities of the children of Israel, and all their transgressions, even all their sins; and *he shall put them upon the head of the goat*, and shall send him away by the hand of a man that is in readiness into the wilderness: and *the goat shall bear upon him all their iniquities* unto a solitary land.'

4. In the execution of the guilty or the trial of the accused:

Lev. xxiv. 14 ('Bring forth him that hath cursed without the camp; and let all that heard him lay their hands upon his head, and let all the congregation stone him'), Susanna 34. There is a close analogy between the sacrificial victim and the criminal. Both are looked upon as representative. On both the sin of the community is regarded as concentrated (comp. Josh. vii. 1). Of this the laying on of hands is the natural symbol. 'When a tribesman is executed for an impious offence, he dies on behalf of the community, to restore normal relations between them and their god; so that the analogy with sacrifice is very close in purpose as well as in form. And so, the cases in which the anger of the god can be traced to the crime of a particular individual, and atoned for by his death, are very naturally seized upon to explain the cases in which the sin of the community cannot be thus individualised, but where, nevertheless, according to ancient custom, reconciliation is sought through the sacrifice of a theanthropic victim' (Robertson Smith *The Religion of the Semites* p. 401).

It should be noticed that in all these passages from the Old Testament except Gen. xlviii. 14 ff. (וַיָּשֶׁת עַל־רֹאשׁ) the verb סמך is used. The word means to lean or rest one thing upon another (*e.g.* Amos v. 19, the hand upon a wall). In the later language the verb סמך has a technical meaning, 'to appoint by laying on of hands'; so a Rabbi made a disciple. The noun סמיכה means 'appointment by the laying of hands.' See Buxtorf *Lex. Chald. Talmud. et Rabbin.* 1498, Schoettgen *Horae Hebr.* i. p. 874 f., ii. p. 887 f.

The idea then expressed in the symbolical act of laying on of hands is the transference of character or of endowment —divine favour, the function of service, official honour and capacity, guilt. Moreover the notion of the unity of tribal or national life is not far in the background. In some cases—the appointment of the Levites, the sacrificial victims (especially the goat in the ritual of the day of Atonement), the condemned criminal—it is prominent. That which belongs to the whole community is concentrated on a representative.

New Testament.

1. In blessing :

Mark x. 16, (‖Matt. xix. 15).

2. In healing the sick :

a. The Lord, *e.g.* Mark v. 23, vi. 5, vii. 32, viii. 23, 25.

β. The disciples, [Mark] xvi. 18, Acts ix. 12, 17 (see above pp. 29 ff.), xxviii. 8.

3. In Confirmation :

Acts viii. 17, 19, xix. 6, 2 Tim. i. 6 (see above pp. 35 ff.), Hebr. vi. 2.

4. In Absolution :

1 Tim. v. 22. The passage is commonly taken to refer to Ordination ; and for this interpretation there is ancient authority. But the sequence of ideas seems to imply that the laying on of hands spoken of is a symbol of absolution and restoration[1].

---

[1] Compare Hort *The Christian Ecclesia* pp. 214 f.

5.   In Ordination or in appointment to some special work of ministry :

Acts vi. 6, xiii. 3, 1 Tim. iv. 14.

In the New Testament as in the Old the idea embodied in the laying on of hands is the transference of character or endowment, divine favour, health bodily or spiritual, the gift of the Spirit, authority and *charismata* for ministry.   In the New Testament as in the Old the thought of corporate life must not be dissociated from the laying on of hands; only now the catholic society, the brotherhood of the Redeemed, has taken the place of the nation.   In all cases (for our Lord Himself was 'sent' by the Father) the final source of blessing is God the Father.   The man who lays hands on another is the outward and visible channel of blessing.   He who so acts does so in relation to his membership in the Spirit-bearing body, the Church.   The endowment of which he is the channel is a share in the endowment which belongs to the whole Christian society as such.

II. *Anointing.*

Old Testament.

The religious use of unction in the Old Testament is an extension of its social use in the life of the East. Unction followed the bath (Ruth iii. 3). The host anoints his guests for their comfort and as a sign of his welcome and good will (comp. 2 Chron. xxviii. 15, Luke vii. 46). Anointing is regarded as the antithesis of mourning or fasting when life is bereft of its dignity and completeness (2 Sam. xii. 20, Amos vi. 6, Dan. x. 3; comp. Matt. vi. 17). Unction therefore is the symbol of prosperity and fulness of gladness and of strength (Ps. xcii. 10, Prov. xxvii. 9, Eccles. ix. 8). Oil is one of God's gifts for man's happiness. (Judg. ix. 9, Ps. civ. 15).

When we turn to the religious use of unction, we note that, by a metaphor drawn from human hospitality, God is said to anoint those whom He regards with favour and to whom He is pleased to grant His blessing (Ps. xxiii. 5, xlv. 7). So Prophets are metaphorically described as anointed

(1 Kings xix. 16, Ps. cv. 15 ; comp. Is. lxi. 1 'The spirit of the Lord God is upon me; because the Lord hath anointed me'). In regard to two classes of officers in the theocracy the outward symbol of unction was used—the High Priest (Lev. viii. 12, Ps. cxxxiii. 2, Ecclus. xlv. 15) and the king (*e.g.* 1 Sam. xvi. 13 'Samuel...anointed [David] in the midst of his brethren ; and the spirit of the Lord came mightily upon David from that day forward').

The ideas therefore involved in religious anointing are (1) divine favour; (2) the bestowal of the divine gift of fulness of life and power ; and this gift is in two passages regarded as 'the spirit of Jehovah'; (3) consequently consecration to God and His service, as the guest is bound to his host by ties of hospitality.

New Testament.

Anointing is mentioned in the following connexions :

(1) Hospitality :
Luke vii. 46.

(2) Healing :

(*a*) Luke x. 34, Apoc. iii. 18.

(*b*) John ix. 6, 11 (πηλὸν ἐποίησεν καὶ ἐπέχρισέν μου τοὺς ὀφθαλμούς) ; comp. Mark vii. 33, viii. 23.

(*c*) Mark vi. 13, Jas. v. 14.

(3) The gift of the Holy Spirit :

(*a*) Christ : Luke iv. 18 (Is. lxi. 1), Acts iv. 27, x. 38 ; comp. Hebr. i. 9 (Ps. xlv. 7).

(*b*) Christians : 2 Cor. i. 21 f., 1 John ii. 20, 27.

In the last group of passages (3) the fulness of life and power is embodied in the personal Holy Spirit ; comp. *e.g.* John vi. 63 (τὸ πνεῦμα τὸ ζωοποιοῦν).

III. *Passages of the Apostolic Epistles which speak of the definite bestowal of the Holy Spirit.*

It remains still to consider those passages of the New Testament which speak of a definite historical bestowal of the Holy

Spirit upon members of the Church but do not mention any outward or visible sign. In these passages the language employed, especially the use of the aorist, seems to shew plainly that the writer has in mind a special crisis in the past, a crisis which in some cases the context connects explicitly with the beginning of the Christian life. It is clear that these passages must be considered in the light of the historical and representative narratives of the Acts (viii. 15 ff., xix. 6), of 2 Tim. i. 6 f., and of Heb. vi. 2, 4.

(1) The Epistle of St James, probably the earliest Christian writing which has come down to us.

iv. 5 ἢ δοκεῖτε ὅτι κενῶς ἡ γραφὴ λέγει Πρὸς φθόνον ἐπιποθεῖ τὸ πνεῦμα ὃ κατῴκισεν ἐν ἡμῖν; These somewhat difficult words seem to mean 'Or think ye that the Scripture saith in vain The Spirit which he made to dwell in us yearneth over us enviously?' St James appears to condense into a single Christianized saying the teaching of those passages in the Old Testament which speak of God's jealousy over His people. Compare *e.g.* Ex. xx. 5, Deut. xxxii. 16, Is. lxiii. 10 ('But they rebelled and grieved his holy spirit'). We are now however only concerned with the words τὸ πνεῦμα ὃ κατῴκισεν ἐν ἡμῖν. The aorist κατῴκισεν, 'caused to make his abiding home in us' (comp. Rom. viii. 9, 11, 1 Cor. iii. 16, vi. 19, 2 Cor. vi. 16), points back to a clearly marked season in God's dealing with believers. For, though the Epistle is addressed to 'the twelve tribes which are in the Dispersion' (i. 1), yet in two other crucial passages 'us' and 'our' refer to Christians as such (i. 18, ii. 1)[1]. It is not easy to decide whether the ἐν ἡμῖν regards Christians as a society or as individuals; whether, in other words, the allusion is to the gift of the Spirit given at Pentecost to the whole Church[2] or to the same gift pledged to each several Christian in Confirmation. It may with some force be urged that the word ἐπιποθεῖ, denoting the relation of the Holy Spirit to the individual

---

[1] In ii. 21 the Apostle writing as a Jew to Jews speaks of 'Abraham our father.' In iii. 3, 6, v. 17 the ἡμῖν, ἡμῶν, ἡμῖν are quite unemphatic and refer to *us men*.

[2] Comp. 1 Pet. i. 12 ἃ νῦν ἀνηγγέλη ὑμῖν διὰ τῶν εὐαγγελισαμένων ὑμᾶς πνεύματι ἁγίῳ ἀποσταλέντι ἀπ' οὐρανοῦ.

Christian (comp. μὴ λυπεῖτε τὸ πνεῦμα τὸ ἅγιον τοῦ θεοῦ Eph. iv. 30), points to the latter interpretation. But in truth the two interpretations are so closely akin that perhaps we are not bound sharply to distinguish between them.

(2) St Paul's Epistles.

(i) First group: the two Epistles to the Thessalonians.

1 Thessalonians i. 6 δεξάμενοι τὸν λόγον ἐν θλίψει πολλῇ μετὰ χαρᾶς πνεύματος ἁγίου.

iv. 7 f. οὐ γὰρ ἐκάλεσεν ἡμᾶς ὁ θεὸς ἐπὶ ἀκαθαρσίᾳ ἀλλ' ἐν ἁγιασμῷ. τοιγαροῦν ὁ ἀθετῶν οὐκ ἄνθρωπον ἀθετεῖ ἀλλὰ τὸν θεὸν τὸν διδόντα τὸ πνεῦμα αὐτοῦ τὸ ἅγιον εἰς ὑμᾶς (Ezek. xxxvii. 14).

2 Thessalonians ii. 13 εἵλατο ὑμᾶς ὁ θεὸς ἀπ' ἀρχῆς [v. l. ἀπαρχὴν] εἰς σωτηρίαν ἐν ἁγιασμῷ πνεύματος καὶ πίστει ἀληθείας, εἰς ὃ ἐκάλεσεν ὑμᾶς διὰ τοῦ εὐαγγελίου ἡμῶν.

In these passages St Paul connects operations of the Holy Spirit (χαρά, ἁγιασμός) with the 'call' of the Thessalonians. The Holy Spirit, then bestowed upon them, inspired them with joy (comp. Gal. v. 22, Rom. xiv. 17) and made them holy (comp. 1 Pet. i. 2, 1 Cor. iii. 16 f., vi. 19). This thought of the definite bestowal of the Holy Spirit in the first days of their discipleship, which is implied in the Apostle's words, would be still further emphasized if in 1 iv. 8 the reading δόντα (comp. Acts xi. 17, xv. 8, 2 Cor. i. 22, v. 5, 2 Tim. i. 7, 1 John iii. 24) were the better supported reading. But the present participle διδόντα is no doubt the true reading. Dr Milligan *in loco* takes τὸν διδόντα as a substantive participle, 'the giver of His Holy Spirit'; but the added words εἰς ὑμᾶς is against this interpretation. Probably Bishop Lightfoot's comment *in loco* is correct, '*i.e.* who is ever renewing this witness against uncleanness in fresh accessions of the Holy Spirit' (comp. 1 Cor. vi. 19 οὗ ἔχετε ἀπὸ θεοῦ). There is precisely the same sequence of thought in Gal. iii. 2, 5 τὸ πνεῦμα ἐλάβετε...ὁ οὖν ἐπιχορηγῶν ὑμῖν τὸ πνεῦμα. St Paul's phrase is indeed an important warning against a rigid and mechanical view of God's dealings with men. To the Christian the Holy Spirit is at once a definite gift in the past (comp. 2 Tim. i. 6) and an ever fresh gift in the present[1].

(ii) Second group: 1, 2 Corinthians, Galatians, Romans.

1 Corinthians ii. 12 ἡμεῖς δὲ οὐ τὸ πνεῦμα τοῦ κόσμου ἐλάβομεν ἀλλὰ τὸ πνεῦμα τὸ ἐκ τοῦ θεοῦ, ἵνα εἰδῶμεν τὰ ὑπὸ τοῦ θεοῦ χαρισθέντα ἡμῖν. Who are the 'we' (ἡμεῖς)? The teachers of the Church or the members of the Church as such? I believe that a careful study of the whole context shews that the latter is the true interpretation. In the preceding context (v. 7), for example, St Paul has spoken of a 'hidden' 'wisdom of God,' 'which God foreordained before the ages for our glory' (εἰς δόξαν ἡμῶν). It is impossible to suppose that the Apostle here speaks of 'the glory' of himself and his fellow-teachers; he must refer to 'the glory' of all the faithful. Throughout the passage he describes the essential position of all

---

[1] Compare ὁ καλέσας Gal. i. 6, 15, 2 Tim. i. 9, 1 Pet. i. 15, v. 10; ὁ καλῶν 1 Thess. v. 24, Gal. v. 8. In 1 Thess. ii. 12 the true reading (καλοῦντος or καλέσαντος) is somewhat doubtful. He who 'called' ever repeats the 'call'; it is 'new every morning.'

believers, though many do not themselves
realize the position which is theirs by right
(iii. 1 f.). All believers ideally are not
'natural men' (ψυχικοί) but 'spiritual men'
(πνευματικοί), who can sift, appraise,
judge all things—ὁ δὲ πνευματικὸς ἀνακρίνει
μὲν πάντα (v. 15). The point of his rebuke
of the Corinthian Brethren lies in this, that
they were content to fall so far below the
character which was theirs as Christians.
This character was theirs, they were
'spiritual men,' because when they became
believers, when (to use Bishop Lightfoot's
phrase *in loco*) they 'were admitted to the
fold of Christ,' they 'received' (ἐλάβομεν)
'the Spirit which is from God.' The
reference, it will be observed, is quite
definite. It is explained when we compare
St Paul's question to the disciples at
Ephesus seen in the light of the subsequent
history (Acts xix. 2 ff.)—εἰ πνεῦμα ἅγιον
ἐλάβετε πιστεύσαντες; The Corinthians
'received the Spirit' when, having been
baptised, they were confirmed by the laying
on of hands. There were then Confirma-
tions at Corinth as there was a Confirmation at Ephesus. St Paul, it must be

noted, is here emphasizing one special aspect of the Pentecostal or Confirmation gift. The Spirit bestowed is the 'Spirit of wisdom and revelation' (πνεῦμα σοφίας καὶ ἀποκαλύψεως, Eph. i. 17). Above (vv. 9 f.), in reference to 'whatsoever things God prepared for them that love him,' he had said 'to us [i.e. to us Christians] God revealed (ἀπεκάλυψεν) them through the Spirit[1].' Later (v. 12) he again emphasizes the same thought, 'We received the Spirit which is from God; that we might know the things that were freely given to us by God,' the blessings, that is, bestowed on us 'in Christ.' The Spirit interprets Christ to the Christian and unfolds the meaning of the gifts which are summed up in the supreme Gift. Compare John xiv. 16 (τὸ πνεῦμα τῆς ἀληθείας), 26 (διδάξει πάντα), xv. 26, xvi. 13 (ὁδηγήσει ὑμᾶς εἰς τὴν ἀλήθειαν πᾶσαν), 1 John ii. 20 f., 27 (see above pp. 58 f.).

1 Corinthians vi. 11 καὶ ταῦτά τινες ἦτε·

---

[1] Compare Bp Lightfoot's note *in loco*, 'The aorist (ἀπεκάλυ-ψεν) is on a par with many aorists in St Paul. Its force is "revealed it to us when we were admitted into the Church, when we were baptised."' This is true if we regard Confirmation as included in Baptism.

ἀλλὰ ἀπελούσασθε, ἀλλὰ ἡγιάσθητε, ἀλλὰ ἐδικαιώθητε ἐν τῷ ὀνόματι τοῦ κυρίου ἡμῶν Ἰησοῦ Χριστοῦ καὶ ἐν τῷ πνεύματι τοῦ θεοῦ ἡμῶν. The Apostle has just said that sinners as such shall not 'inherit the kingdom of God,' and has enumerated types of sinners such as were common in the pagan world, common in a centre of commerce and of pleasure like Corinth. Then he turns to his converts. 'Such characters in some sort were ye'. But ye washed; ye were made holy; ye were acquitted.' In the ἀπελούσασθε there is a clear reference to Baptism; compare Acts xxii. 16 ἀναστὰς βάπτισαι καὶ ἀπόλουσαι τὰς ἁμαρτίας σου. The ἡγιάσθητε, following the ἀπελούσασθε as the next step in the great process of renewal, contains a no less clear allusion to the gift of the sanctifying Spirit in Confirmation. For sanctification (ἁγιασμός) in sharp contrast to the ἀκαθαρσία of heathen life compare 1 Thess. iv. 7. This

---

[1] The rendering 'Such were some of you,' A.V. and R.V., is indefensible. The τινες softens the ταῦτα; compare τοιοῦτός τις. See Field's *Notes on the Translation of the New Testament*, p. 172. Field quotes Chrysostom's comment (xi. 25 E): οὐκ εἶπεν ἀπλῶς, ἦτε, ἀλλά, τινες ἦτε· τουτέστιν, οὕτω πως ἦτε.

'washing away' of past sins and this bestowal by God of a new positive character of holiness together constituted an outward and visible sentence of acquittal. This interpretation is confirmed by the words which follow ἐν τῷ ὀνόματι τοῦ κυρίου ἡμῶν Ἰησοῦ Χριστοῦ καὶ ἐν τῷ πνεύματι τοῦ θεοῦ ἡμῶν. The passage has taken the form of a rhetorical climax. The thrice repeated ἀλλά before each of the three verbs marks forcibly the three stages. To introduce the supplementary words ἐν τῷ ὀνόματι κ.τ.λ. before the close would have broken up the rhetorical compactness of the sentence; they are added therefore as an important appendix. But the ἐν τῷ ὀνόματι specially refers back to the ἀπελούσασθε; for these converts had been baptised 'into the name of Jesus Christ,' 'into Christ.' The ἐν τῷ πνεύματι specially refers back to the ἡγιάσθητε; compare 2 Thess. ii. 13, Rom. xv. 16, 1 Pet. i. 2. The sequence of thought is thus exactly parallel to that in Titus iii. 5 ff., ἔσωσεν...διὰ λουτροῦ παλινγενεσίας καὶ ἀνακαινώσεως πνεύματος ἁγίου...ἵνα δικαιωθέντες κ.τ.λ. Converts who had been cleansed in Baptism and who had received

the visible token of the gift of the sanctifying Spirit could point to an effectual sign
of their acquittal from the sins which had
defiled their past life.

1 Corinthians xii. 13 καὶ γὰρ ἐν ἑνὶ πνεύματι ἡμεῖς πάντες εἰς ἓν σῶμα ἐβαπτίσθημεν,
εἴτε Ἰουδαῖοι εἴτε Ἕλληνες, εἴτε δοῦλοι εἴτε
ἐλεύθεροι, καὶ πάντες ἓν πνεῦμα ἐποτίσθη-
μεν. St Paul in the preceding words has
spoken of the one body and the many
members. 'So also,' he adds, 'is the
Christ,' the ascended and glorified Christ.
He proceeds to justify the relevancy of
his assertion, adding at the same time a
new thought (καὶ γάρ). The new thought
is the thought of the Spirit. Every living
human body is ruled and guided by a spirit;
so it is with the 'new man,' 'the Christ.'
Baptism is the incorporation of the baptised
into the one Body permeated and transfused
by the one Spirit (comp. Eph. iv. 4).
The relevancy of the conception of the
Christ as the Body with many members
lies in the fact that all Christians by their
Baptism were incorporated into that one
Body and were brought within the control
of the one Spirit, who quickens and

directs all the members. But that is not
all. Christians were not only by Baptism
brought within the sphere of the operation
of the Spirit. Their Baptism was followed
by ($\dot{\epsilon}\beta\alpha\pi\tau\dot{\iota}\sigma\theta\eta\mu\epsilon\nu\ldots\kappa\alpha\dot{\iota}\ldots\dot{\epsilon}\pi\sigma\tau\dot{\iota}\sigma\theta\eta\mu\epsilon\nu$) a
reception of the Spirit. This reception
St Paul describes by a metaphor drawn
from the story of Israel, to which he had
referred in an earlier passage (x. 4), and
the thought of which still lingers in his
mind. At Rephidim (Exod. xvii. 6; comp.
Numb. xx. 8 ff.) the Israelites drank of the
water which flowed from the rock. The
rock was an allegory—a 'spiritual rock,'
'the Christ.' The stream also which
flowed from it was an allegory—'spiritual
drink,' the Holy Spirit which is the gift of
the Father through 'the Christ.' 'We
were all made to drink of one Spirit'
(comp. John vii. 37 ff.). The particular
metaphor chosen enables St Paul to suggest
the thought that the gift of the Spirit
had refreshed and invigorated those who
had long and hopelessly traversed the
wilderness of ignorance and sin. This
reception of the Spirit was closely associated with Baptism, yet it was not identical

with Baptism. It has a distinct place of its own in the Apostle's account of the initial stage of the Christian life (πάντες). When we compare his words here with the typical history of his dealings with converts (Acts xix. 5 f.), we cannot doubt that the reference here is to the gift of the Holy Spirit in Confirmation.

2 Corinthians i. 21 f. ὁ δὲ βεβαιῶν ἡμᾶς σὺν ὑμῖν εἰς Χριστὸν καὶ χρίσας ἡμᾶς θεός, ὁ καὶ σφραγισάμενος ἡμᾶς καὶ δοὺς τὸν ἀρραβῶνα τοῦ πνεύματος ἐν ταῖς καρδίαις ἡμῶν. St Paul has just protested against the charge of fickleness which had been brought against him (v. 17). His message was not an alternation of 'yea' and 'nay' (v. 17). For neither is such the character of Him who was the centre of that message, 'the Son of God Christ Jesus' (v. 19). 'In Him' is the affirmation (τὸ Ναί) 'of all the promises of God,' and therefore 'through Him' is their ratification and fulfilment (τὸ Ἀμήν) (v. 20). The thought of this ratification of the promises suggests at once to the Apostle's mind (1) the word βεβαιοῦν; comp. Rom. xv. 8 εἰς τὸ βεβαιῶσαι τὰς ἐπαγγελίας τῶν πατέρων:

(2) the idea of the divine confirmation not of promises only but of men. 'It is God who confirmeth us missionaries and you converts alike, bringing us into union with Christ.' This divine process of confirmation springs out of the supreme gift of the Holy Spirit once for all given 'to us and to you.' God 'anointed' us—the εἰς Χριστόν leads on to the χρίσας; He 'sealed' us; He put the Spirit into our hearts who is the pledge of all divine gifts (comp. Eph. i. 14 ἀρραβὼν τῆς κληρονομίας ἡμῶν). Two points must be noted. (i) Some commentators take the 'us' and 'our'—χρίσας ἡμᾶς, σφραγισάμενος ἡμᾶς, ἐν ταῖς καρδίαις ἡμῶν—to refer to the missionaries. This is unnecessary after the 'us with you'—ὁ δὲ βεβαιῶν ἡμᾶς σὺν ὑμῖν; incredible when we compare other Pauline passages—2 Cor. v. 5, Eph. i. 14, iv. 30 where similar language is used in regard to Christian people generally. (ii) The transition from the present participle (βεβαιῶν) to the three aorist participles (χρίσας, σφραγισάμενος, δούς) marks clearly

---

[1] Compare Eph. i. 12 ἡμᾶς ('us Jews'); v. 13 ἐν ᾧ καὶ ὑμεῖς ('you Gentiles'); v. 14 τῆς κληρονομίας ἡμῶν ('ours both Jews and Gentiles').

that the Apostle has in mind a bestowal of the Spirit which lay in the past, when the Corinthian Christians became believers (Eph. i. 14). We have already seen (see above pp. 51 ff., 57 f.) that in χρίσας and σφραγισάμενος we probably have an allusion to outward signs used in Confirmation.

2 Corinthians v. 5 ὁ δὲ κατεργασάμενος ἡμᾶς εἰς αὐτὸ τοῦτο θεός, ὁ δοὺς ἡμῖν τὸν ἀρραβῶνα τοῦ πνεύματος. In the previous verse St Paul has spoken of the goal of being to which he looks forward—ἵνα καταποθῇ τὸ θνητὸν ὑπὸ τῆς ζωῆς—life absorbing into itself, transmuting into itself, all that is mortal in the man. 'Now,' he adds, 'he who wrought us for this very thing is God.' For the thought we compare Eph. ii. 10 αὐτοῦ γάρ ἐσμεν ποίημα, κτισθέντες ἐν Χριστῷ 'Ἰησοῦ. The reference is to the spiritual re-creation of each man, outwardly and visibly consummated in his Baptism. He then continues 'who gave us the earnest of the Spirit.' For the definite reference in this phrase to Confirmation see above on i. 22. The Spirit then given to each man is the pledge of his final renewal and of his immortality. In

Rom. viii. 11—ζωοποιήσει καὶ τὰ θνητὰ σώματα ὑμῶν διὰ τοῦ ἐνοικοῦντος αὐτοῦ πνεύματος (*v. l.* διὰ τὸ ἐνοικοῦν αὐτοῦ πνεῦμα) ἐν ὑμῖν—the thought is very similar; but in this latter passage St Paul has in mind the perpetual indwelling of the Spirit, which is the outcome of the initial gift ; and he regards the Spirit not as the pledge but as the means, or, if we adopt the alternative reading, as the cause, of the future and final quickening.

2 Corinthians xi. 4 εἰ μὲν γὰρ ὁ ἐρχόμενος ἄλλον Ἰησοῦν κηρύσσει ὃν οὐκ ἐκηρύξαμεν, ἢ πνεῦμα ἕτερον λαμβάνετε ὃ οὐκ ἐλάβετε...καλῶς ἀνέχεσθε (*v. l.* ἀνείχεσθε). St Paul fears the seduction of his converts at Corinth from their pledged loyalty to the Christ (*v.* 3). 'For if indeed,' he continues in bitter irony, 'the teacher who visits you is preaching another Jesus whom we did not preach, or if ye are receiving a different Spirit whom ye did not receive...this is indeed a noble tolerance of yours.' The ἐκηρύξαμεν points back to the time of the conversion of the Corinthians. The reference in πνεῦμα ἕτερον ὃ οὐκ ἐλάβετε is again quite definite, *i.e.*, to

their reception of the Spirit at that :
their Confirmation (comp. Acts xix. 2

Galatians iii. 2 ff. ἐξ ἔργων νόμου τὸ
πνεῦμα ἐλάβετε ἢ ἐξ ἀκοῆς πίστεως; ἐν-
αρξάμενοι πνεύματι νῦν σαρκὶ ἐπιτελεῖσθε;
...ὁ οὖν ἐπιχορηγῶν ὑμῖν τὸ πνεῦμα καὶ
ἐνεργῶν δυνάμεις ἐν ὑμῖν ἐξ ἔργων νόμου ἢ
ἐξ ἀκοῆς πίστεως; The Galatians were in
danger of lapsing into a formal lifeless
legalism. St Paul points them to the fatal
contradiction between the position in which
they were now placing themselves and
their original position which had received
the seal of divine approval. Then they
did not rely on works done in bondage to
the Law, but on faith which led them to
hear and obey the proclamation of the
Gospel (comp. Rom. i. 5, xvi. 26). To
that faith of theirs God had responded by
the gift of the Spirit. They believed;
therefore they received the Spirit (comp.
Acts xix. 2). Clearly St Paul refers to a
reception of the Spirit to which they could
look back as a definite and clearly marked,
an outward and visible, crisis in their
lives. This remembrance leads him to
speak of a second contradiction between

their past and their present. Nothing lower than the Spirit dominated the beginning of their Christian life. Nothing higher than the flesh dominated the supposed perfecting of their Christian life, of which they now boasted. They were in fact exchanging their Pentecostal life in the Spirit for a legal life in the flesh. After an allusion to the frustration of their earlier sufferings for the sake of Christ involved in their retrograde movement. St Paul resumes (οὖν) his question as to efficacy of faith and of works. But the question takes a new form and that in two directions. First he concentrates his thought on the divine side, on God as the giver of the Spirit. Secondly he turns from the historical scene of their reception of the Spirit to the continued bounty of God in the bestowal of the Spirit (ὁ ἐπιχορηγῶν: comp. Phil. i. 19)[1]. That bounty is God's recognition not of man's works but of man's faith. Such seems to be the sequence of thought in the passage. We are now concerned with the words τὸ

[1] On the relation of ὁ ἐπιχορηγῶν to ἐλάβετε see above pp. 73 f.

πνεῦμα ἐλάβετε. We learn from them that, when St Paul planted the Gospel there, there were Confirmation scenes in Galatia. Further, we infer the importance which St Paul attached to Confirmation. He appeals to it as involving a standard of the life which followed it.

Galatians iv. 6 f. ὅτι δέ ἐστε υἱοί, ἐξαπέστειλεν ὁ θεὸς τὸ πνεῦμα τοῦ υἱοῦ αὐτοῦ εἰς τὰς καρδίας ἡμῶν, κρᾶζον ᾿Αββά ὁ πατήρ. ὥστε οὐκέτι εἶ δοῦλος ἀλλὰ υἱός, εἰ δὲ υἱός καὶ κληρονόμος, διὰ θεοῦ. In the Christian dispensation there are two supreme Missions, the Mission of the Son and the Mission of the Spirit: 'God sent forth (ἐξαπέστειλεν) his Son'; 'God sent forth (ἐξαπέστειλεν) the Spirit.' In the preceding verse St Paul has spoken of the Mission of the Son and its purpose—'that we might receive the adoption of sons.' 'In Him' we are sons. The Mission of the Son was definite; it had its place among the events of history. The Apostle now passes on to speak of the Mission of the Spirit. That also was historical. The Day of Pentecost, like the day of the Saviour's birth, had its place in the annals of human history.

Here however he regards that historical Mission of the Spirit as it is historically rehearsed and applied in the case of individual Christians—'God sent forth the Spirit of his Son *into our hearts*.' Confirmation, as we have already said (see above p. 21), is the Pentecost of the individual soul. That is the thought which finds expression here. St Paul is enforcing here one aspect of the Mission of the Spirit. He is 'the Spirit of adoption' (Rom. viii. 15). He is the seal of sonship and the means of the realization of sonship. He makes the sense of sonship articulate in the believer (κρᾶζον 'Αββά ὁ πατήρ). Hence the remarkable description of the Holy Spirit as 'the Spirit of his Son.' The Spirit, who witnesses of their sonship to those who are 'in Christ,' is Himself the Spirit of the Eternal Son, sent by the Father through the mediation of the Son. His office in the Church is, if we may venture so to express it, rooted in His eternal Being, in His eternal relation to the Father and the Son. In the last verse (ὥστε οὐκέτι κ.τ.λ.) St Paul sums up the result of the two Missions, the Mission of the Son and the

Mission of the Spirit, and presents that result as the possession of each individual Christian. The relation of each man to God as a bondservant is henceforth obliterated. He who is 'in Christ' is a son, an heir, of God, the thought of heirship introducing the idea of the boundless future possibilities of God's purpose for His sons. If I mistake not, the διὰ θεοῦ refers not to κληρονόμος alone but to υἱός and κληρονόμος. It takes up emphatically at the close of the paragraph, the thought of the twice-repeated ἐξαπέστειλεν ὁ θεός. Man is constituted son and heir not by his own deserts but by the direct interposition of God Himself[1].

Romans i. 11 f. ἐπιποθῶ γὰρ ἰδεῖν ὑμᾶς, ἵνα τι μεταδῶ χάρισμα ὑμῖν πνευματικὸν εἰς τὸ στηριχθῆναι ὑμᾶς, τοῦτο δέ ἐστιν συνπαρακληθῆναι ἐν ὑμῖν διὰ τῆς ἐν ἀλλήλοις πίστεως ὑμῶν τε καὶ ἐμοῦ. If we take into account the typical narrative of St Luke (Acts xix. 2), it appears at least possible that St Paul looked forward to a like exercise of his Apostolic ministry at

---

[1] To indicate this thought I have ventured slightly to alter the punctuation of Westcott and Hort's text.

Rome. The language used is patient of this interpretation. St Paul does not say ἵνα μεταδῶ χαρίσματα ὑμῖν πνευματικά (comp. 1 Cor. xii. 1, 4, Rom. xii. 6). He has some one definite χάρισμα πνευματικόν in mind. The τι separated from the substantive and adjective is by position slightly prominent. The word χάρισμα in 2 Tim. i. 6 (see above pp. 35 ff.) is used of the 'inward and spiritual grace' in Confirmation. The phrase εἰς τὸ στηριχθῆναι ὑμᾶς very well suits this interpretation. Though στηρίζειν is not elsewhere in the New Testament[1] specially used in relation to Confirmation, yet it naturally and appropriately expresses the result of Confirmation—the strengthening and compacting of the spiritual character. Nor do the words which follow strike a different note. In them St Paul guards against seeming to describe himself simply as a benefactor: he will receive as well as give. He and his friends at Rome alike will be encouraged (συνπαρακληθῆναι[2]), they by his

---

[1] See 1 Thess. iii. 2, 13, 2 Thess. ii. 17, iii. 3, Rom. xvi. 25; Acts xviii. 23; 1 Pet. v. 10; ἐπιστηρίζειν Acts xiv. 22, xv. 32, 41.

[2] For the juxtaposition of στηρίζειν and παρακαλεῖν comp. Acts xiv. 22, xv. 32, 1 Thess. iii. 2, 2 Thess. ii. 17.

faith and he by their faith—their faith deepened and invigorated by the Holy Spirit (1 Cor. xii. 9). The language of the passage is not indeed decisive; but, when it is read in the light of St Paul's action at Ephesus, it appears naturally to suggest that he looked forward to visiting the Church at Rome, which had not been either planted or watered by any one of the Apostles, that he might exercise his apostolic ministry among the Christians there and might give them the seal of the Spirit[1].

Romans v. 5 ἡ ἀγάπη τοῦ θεοῦ ἐκκέχυται ἐν ταῖς καρδίαις ἡμῶν διὰ πνεύματος ἁγίου τοῦ δοθέντος ἡμῖν. We notice the aorist τοῦ δοθέντος with its definite reference to the beginning of the Christian life. The Holy Spirit once given is the means whereby the love of God also is abundantly

---

[1] The rendering of the passage in the Syriac Vulgate, the Peshitta, implies this interpretation—'Because I am greatly desiring to see you and to give you the gift of the Spirit, that by it ye may be strengthened and together we may be comforted by the faith of you and of me.' Bengel's note *in loco* is instructive—'Talibus donis abundabant Corinthii, qui Paulum praesentem habuerant: 1 Cor. i. 7, xii. 1, xiv. 1, nec non Galatae, Gal. iii. 5. Ac plane ecclesiae illae, quae *apostolorum praesentia* gaudebant, praerogativas insignes in hoc genere habuere, v. gr. ex apostolica manuum impositione. Act. xix. 2, 6, viii. 17 s., 2 Tim. i. 6.' The last reference should be noted (see above pp. 35 ff.).

bestowed and made to dwell in the hearts of believers. St Paul in reference to God's love given through the Spirit uses the Pentecostal keyword (see above p. 22 n.).

Romans viii. 14 ff. ὅσοι γὰρ πνεύματι θεοῦ ἄγονται, οὗτοι υἱοὶ θεοῦ εἰσίν. οὐ γὰρ ἐλάβετε πνεῦμα δουλείας πάλιν εἰς φόβον, ἀλλὰ ἐλάβετε πνεῦμα υἱοθεσίας, ἐν ᾧ κράζομεν ᾿Αββά ὁ πατήρ· αὐτὸ τὸ πνεῦμα συνμαρτυρεῖ τῷ πνεύματι ἡμῶν ὅτι ἐσμὲν τέκνα θεοῦ· εἰ δὲ τέκνα καὶ κληρονόμοι· κληρονόμοι μὲν θεοῦ, συνκληρονόμοι δὲ Χριστοῦ, εἴπερ συνπάσχομεν ἵνα καὶ συνδοξασθῶμεν. For ἄγονται compare Luke iv. 1 ἤγετο ἐν τῷ πνεύματι ἐν τῇ ἐρήμῳ. St Paul in this passage dwells on the same thoughts as he had already expressed in Gal. iv. 6 f. (see above pp. 87 ff.). In the ἐλάβετε (comp. 1 Cor. ii. 12 ; see above p. 25) he has in view Confirmation. In Gal. *l. c.* he refers to the action of God (ἐξαπέστειλεν ὁ θεὸς...εἰς τὰς καρδίας ἡμῶν); here to the Christian's reception and possession of the gift. Here accordingly he dwells on the Christian's appeal to God as Father (κράζομεν), prompted and inspired by the Spirit, and on the response of the human spirit to the Spirit's witness as to the relation of the Christian to God as His child. It will be noticed also that τέκνα here takes the place of υἱοί (Gal. *l. c.*), pointing to the divine act of spiritual generation[1] and to the abiding spiritual consequences in him who has been 'begotten again unto a living hope.' This relation of the believer to God carries with it the reality of heirship—'heirs of God'; and this heirship is seen to involve a participation in the divine destiny (if we may so speak) of Christ Himself; the final end being, through fellowship in Christ's sufferings, fellowship in Christ's glory (comp. *vv.* 29, 30). Thus St Paul here traces the eternal significance of the divine Gift. The Christian man 'received' the Spirit. The Spirit inspires the assurance of the Fatherhood of God; the Christian is God's 'child.' He is constituted therefore in union with Christ God's heir. He will share in Christ's eternal 'glory.' The thought finds another expression in a later passage of this chapter—τὴν ἀπαρχὴν τοῦ

---

[1] Comp. 1 Pet. i. 3, 23, John i. 12 f., iii. 3—8, 1 John ii. 29, iii. 9, iv. 7, v. 1, 4, 18.

πνεύματος ἔχοντες (*v.* 23). As the 'firstfruit'
is the promise of the ingathering of the
harvest, so the Spirit 'received' and
possessed in the present is the pledge of
a larger and richer operation of the same
Spirit in the future—the complete realization of 'the adoption as sons,' 'the redemption of the body,' when 'He who
raised up Christ Jesus from the dead shall
quicken also the mortal bodies' of Christian
men 'by his Spirit who dwelleth' in them
(*v.* 11).

(iii)   Third group: Philippians, Coloss-
ians, Philemon, Ephesians.

Ephesians i. 13 f. ἐν ᾧ καὶ ὑμεῖς
ἀκούσαντες τὸν λόγον τῆς ἀληθείας, τὸ εὐαγγέλιον τῆς σωτηρίας ὑμῶν, ἐν ᾧ καὶ
πιστεύσαντες, ἐσφραγίσθητε τῷ πνεύματι
τῆς ἐπαγγελίας τῷ ἁγίῳ, ὅ (*v. l.* ὅς) ἐστιν
ἀρραβὼν τῆς κληρονομίας ἡμῶν, εἰς ἀπολύτρωσιν τῆς περιποιήσεως, εἰς ἔπαινον τῆς
δόξης αὐτοῦ.   The allusion to Confirmation
has been already pointed out (see above
pp. 51 ff.).   St Paul here dwells on two aspects of the gift of the Spirit. (1) That
gift has its relation to the past.   The

Spirit is τὸ πνεῦμα τῆς ἐπαγγελίας.
Compare ii. 12 τῶν διαθηκῶν τῆς ἐπαγγελίας,
iii. 6 τὰ ἔθνη...συμμέτοχα τῆς ἐπαγγελίας
ἐν Χριστῷ Ἰησοῦ. The article (τῆς ἐπαγγελίας) points to the *divine* promise, the
promise of redemption given by God to
Israel. The Spirit poured forth on
Christian men is 'the Spirit of the divine
promise,' the Spirit, that is, whose coming
formed part of, was included in, God's
promise to Israel through the Prophets
(Is. xxxii. 15, Ezek. xi. 19, xxxvi. 26 f.,
xxxvii. 14, xxxix. 29, Joel ii. 28); compare
Luke xxiv. 49, Acts i. 4, ii. 33, 39. St
Paul in the immediately preceding context
had spoken of the relative position of Jew
and of Gentile. 'We Jews were the
first to hope in the Christ' (*v.* 12). In
Christ 'you Gentiles also having heard and
having believed were sealed with the
Spirit, whose Presence was comprehended
in the promise first given by God to us
Jews, in which God now vouchsafes to you
Gentiles to share.' Thus the τῆς ἐπαγγελίας
is closely related to the great theme of the
Epistle: 'He made both one' (ii. 14).
(2) On the other hand the gift has its

relation to the future. The Spirit is 'the earnest of our inheritance.' 'It must be observed,' notes Bishop Lightfoot *in loco*, 'that the expression is not ἐνέχυρον "a pledge," but ἀρραβών "an earnest." In other words the thing given is related to the thing assured—the present to the hereafter—as a part to the whole. It is the same in kind.' The inheritance (comp. Gal. iv. 6 f., Rom. viii. 17), of which the Spirit is the present assurance, is heavenly and spiritual, conditioned and dominated by the Spirit. Thus the phrase here is akin to, but wider than, the ἡ ἀπαρχὴ τοῦ πνεύματος of Rom. viii. 23. The end of the sealing by the Spirit is defined by two parallel clauses. It is 'unto the redemption of God's own possession,' the full and complete emancipation of all God's people whom, like Israel, He has made His own. This thought is expanded in Rom. viii. 21—23. It is also 'unto the praise of His glory' (comp. *vv.* 6, 12), the vindication and the universal acknowledgement of God's perfection. The history of redemption ends in doxology.

Ephesians iv. 30 καὶ μὴ λυπεῖτε τὸ

πνεῦμα τὸ ἅγιον τοῦ θεοῦ, ἐν ᾧ ἐσφραγίσθητε εἰς ἡμέραν ἀπολυτρώσεως. The main thoughts are those of the earlier passage just discussed. But the context is different. There the ideas were personal; here they are those of corporate life—'We are members one of another' (v. 25). Christians in their daily intercourse with their fellow-Christians must ever watch lest they should so act or speak as to grieve (μὴ λυπεῖτε, note the present imperative) the one Spirit (iv. 3 f.), who dwells in all. The μὴ λυπεῖτε brings out the personality of the Spirit. It may be added that probably the phrase ἐν ᾧ ἐσφραγίσθητε (contrasted with the ἐσφραγίσθητε τῷ πνεύματι of the earlier passage) was deliberately used to suggest, in harmony with the context, the thought of incorporation (comp. 1 Cor. xii. 13). We may paraphrase St Paul's words thus 'Be ever vigilant in your dealings with your brethren, lest you grieve the Holy Spirit in whom ye were incorporated and having been incorporated were sealed.' Christians are baptised into the Spirit. In Confirmation they are sealed by the Spirit.

CONFIRMATION IN

(iv) Fourth group: The three Pastoral Epistles.

Titus iii. 4 ff. ὅτε δὲ ἡ χρηστότης καὶ ἡ φιλανθρωπία ἐπεφάνη τοῦ σωτῆρος ἡμῶν θεοῦ, οὐκ ἐξ ἔργων τῶν ἐν δικαιοσύνῃ ἃ ἐποιήσαμεν ἡμεῖς ἀλλὰ κατὰ τὸ αὐτοῦ ἔλεος ἔσωσεν ἡμᾶς διὰ λουτροῦ παλινγενεσίας καὶ ἀνακαινώσεως πνεύματος ἁγίου, οὗ ἐξέχεεν ἐφ’ ἡμᾶς πλουσίως διὰ Ἰησοῦ Χριστοῦ τοῦ σωτῆρος ἡμῶν, ἵνα δικαιωθέντες τῇ ἐκείνου χάριτι κληρονόμοι γενηθῶμεν κατ’ ἐλπίδα ζωῆς αἰωνίου. The passage is by no means free from difficulties of interpretation. (1) What is the construction of the words διὰ λουτροῦ...πνεύματος ἁγίου? Grammatically it is possible to take both παλινγενεσίας and ἀνακαινώσεως in connexion with διὰ λουτροῦ, i.e., 'by the washing[1] of regeneration and of renewal.' But against this construction there are three objections. (i) The phrase λουτρὸν ἀνακαινώσεως πνεύματος ἁγίου is a cumbrous phrase. (ii) If, as in this case is necessary, ἀνακαινώσεως expresses a single definite act of the Holy Spirit, the phrase παλινγενεσίας καὶ ἀνακαινώσεως is open to the

[1] Not 'laver'; see Dean Robinson's note on Eph. v. 26.

charge of tautology; and further, the second word is a weaker word than the first. (iii) The special gift and the consequent operation of the Holy Spirit are not in the New Testament connected with the washing of Baptism. We conclude therefore that the Apostle intends to mark two means of salvation : 'He saved us by the washing of regeneration and by the renewing of the Holy Ghost.' We are led next to ask the question Is the ἀνακαίνωσις a single act or a constant activity of the Holy Spirit? In Rom. xii. 2 (μεταμορφοῦσθε τῇ ἀνακαινώσει τοῦ νοός) a process of renewal is clearly intended (note the present imperative μεταμορφοῦσθε); compare 2 Cor. iv. 16 ὁ ἔσω ἡμῶν [ἄνθρωπος] ἀνακαινοῦται ἡμέρᾳ καὶ ἡμέρᾳ, Col. iii. 10 ἐνδυσάμενοι τὸν νέον [ἄνθρωπον] τὸν ἀνακαινούμενον κ.τ.λ. (where ἐνδυσάμενοι τὸν νέον answers to the παλιγγενεσία of our present passage), Eph. iv. 23 ἀνανεοῦσθαι δὲ τῷ πνεύματι τοῦ νοὸς ὑμῶν. We are therefore safest if, in accordance with the form of the word ἀνακαίνωσις, we understand the phrase διὰ...ἀνακαινώσεως πνεύματος ἁγίου to refer to the continual operation of the Holy

Spirit, though at the same time it is clear from the context (ἔσωσεν...ἐξέχεεν) that St Paul has prominently in his mind the initiation of the process of renewal. (2) What is the time referred to in ἔσωσεν ἡμᾶς? The 'us' appears to be not St Paul and Titus and the flock of Titus but generally 'us Christians' (so in ii. 8, 12, 14, iii. 3). If we had to consider the words by themselves, we might paraphrase them thus 'God brought us into a state of salvation (comp. 1 Pet. iii. 21) when we severally had our part in the washing of regeneration.' But we must take these words in close connexion with the previous clause ὅτε δὲ...ἐπεφάνη. The sequence of clauses is ὅτε ἡ χρηστότης...ἐπεφάνη... ἔσωσεν ἡμᾶς (comp. Gal. iv. 4 ὅτε δὲ ἦλθεν τὸ πλήρωμα τοῦ χρόνου, ἐξαπέστειλεν κ.τ.λ.). 'When the work of redemption was completed by the coming of the Spirit and God's goodness and love towards man were thereby manifested to the world, then in accordance with His mercy, and not because of any works of ours done in a righteousness according to the Law, He brought us Christians into a state of

salvation by means of the washing of
regeneration and the renewing operation
of the Holy Spirit.' It seems to follow
that in the next words οὗ ἐξέχεεν ἐφ' ἡμᾶς
πλουσίως the allusion is to the first outpouring of the Holy Spirit on the day of
Pentecost. For ἐξέχεεν compare Acts ii.
17, 33; in the latter verse the words τήν τε
ἐπαγγελίαν τοῦ πνεύματος τοῦ ἁγίου λαβὼν
παρὰ τοῦ πατρός explain διὰ 'Ιησοῦ Χριστοῦ
τοῦ σωτῆρος ἡμῶν of our present passage.
Thus, when we regard the passage as a
whole, we are led to the conclusion that
St Paul has in mind God's dealings with
the Christian Church rather than with
individual Christians. The reference to
the rite of Confirmation in the words διὰ...
ἀνακαινώσεως πνεύματος ἁγίου οὗ ἐξέχεεν
ἐφ' ἡμᾶς πλουσίως is clear and important,
but it is indirect. Confirmation is the
application of Pentecost to the individual
soul. In the final clause (ἵνα δικαιωθέντες
κ.τ.λ.) St Paul emphasises thoughts which
we have already noticed in an earlier
passage of his writings. Baptism and
Confirmation are the seal of justification or
acquittal; compare 1 Cor. vi. 11 (see above

p. 78). By Baptism and Confirmation the believer is constituted 'an heir, an heir at present so far as hope is concerned, of eternal life'; compare Gal. iv. 7, Rom. viii. 17, Eph. i. 14 (see above pp. 89, 93, 96)[1].

(3)   The Catholic Epistles[2].

1 John ii. 20 f., 27, see above pp. 58 f.

1 John iii. 24 καὶ ἐν τούτῳ γινώσκομεν ὅτι μένει ἐν ἡμῖν, ἐκ τοῦ πνεύματος οὗ ἡμῖν ἔδωκεν. Compare iv. 13 ἐν τούτῳ γινώσκομεν ὅτι ἐν αὐτῷ μένομεν καὶ αὐτὸς ἐν ἡμῖν ὅτι ἐκ τοῦ πνεύματος αὐτοῦ δέδωκεν ἡμῖν. St John here says that the knowledge—the growing and progressive knowledge of experience—that God the Father dwells in us comes from (comp. iv. 6 ἐκ τούτου γινώσκομεν) the Spirit whom He gave us. Christians, the Apostle implies, cannot be mistaken about the presence of the Spirit with them.   They remember the time at

---

[1] I think that it is far more forcible to take ζωῆς αἰωνίου, reserved for solemn emphasis to the end of the sentence, closely with κληρονόμοι; for κληρονομεῖν ζωὴν αἰώνιον see Mark x. 17, Matt. xix. 29, Luke x. 25, xviii. 18.   The κατ' ἐλπίδα qualifies κληρονόμοι γενηθῶμεν; comp. Rom. viii. 24 f.

[2] The passage from the Epistle of St James (iv. 5) has been already considered (see above pp. 70 ff.).

the beginning of their Christian course when God gave them the supreme gift. They then received the pledge of an outward and visible sign. If they faithfully asked for the gift, the pledge was not a vain thing. God did not mock them. With the outward and visible sign they received the inward and spiritual grace; and that grace has not been withdrawn. The Spirit, of whose presence they were and are assured, witnesses to them that the Father Himself dwells in them. In iv. 13—'He hath given us of his Spirit'— St John emphasises the thought that the gift of the Spirit once given abides with the faithful.

The investigation just brought to a close justifies conclusions historical and doctrinal. Some of these I have already pointed out. It will however be convenient to bring them together and to present them in a single statement.

(1)　Historical conclusions.

The writer of the Acts selected, as we saw, typical Confirmation scenes. He only tells us of the two Apostles of the Circumcision, St Peter and St John, confirming disciples at the city of Samaria and of the Apostle of the Gentiles confirming disciples at Ephesus[1]. The Epistles of the New Testament enable us to supplement these representative narratives. The Epistles of St Paul, if our interpretation has been correct, imply that he confirmed Timothy at Lystra during his first missionary journey; that during his second missionary journey he confirmed disciples in the Churches of Galatia, probably at Thessalonica, and at Corinth; that during his third missionary journey he confirmed disciples while sojourning at Ephesus[2]. It is at least a possible inference from his words (Rom. i. 11) that he looked forward

---

[1] Perhaps also of Ananias at Damascus confirming Saul of Tarsus (see above pp. 29 ff.).

[2] The Epistle to the Ephesians was a circular letter to the Churches of Asia Minor. But the language of Acts xx. 18— 'Ye yourselves know, from the first day that I set foot in Asia, how it was with you that I was all the time' ($\pi\hat{\omega}s$ $\mu\epsilon\theta$' $\dot{\upsilon}\mu\hat{\omega}\nu$ $\tau\dot{\omega}\nu$ $\pi\acute{a}\nu\tau a$ $\chi\rho\acute{o}\nu o\nu$ $\dot{\epsilon}\gamma\epsilon\nu\acute{o}\mu\eta\nu$)—shews that while in Asia, St Paul did not visit other cities besides Ephesus.

to confirming disciples at Rome, when he was allowed to pay his long projected visit to the capital of the Empire. It is a reasonable inference from the language which the Apostle uses in his letter to Titus that Confirmation formed part of the ministry of his delegate in Crete. Passing to the other Epistles of the New Testament, we note that the Epistle of St James not improbably affords evidence as to the practice of Confirmation in the Mother Church at Jerusalem; that the Epistle to the Hebrews clearly indicates that Confirmation was familiar to the Hebrew Christians of some Church or of some Churches in Palestine; and that the First Epistle of St John carries on the evidence to the close of the Apostolic age when that Apostle had made his home at Ephesus. It is true that with two exceptions (2 Tim. i. 6 f., Hebr. vi. 1 f.) the passages in the Epistles speak not of the outward rite but of the bestowal of the Holy Spirit on believers. The terms employed however seem plainly to imply that this bestowal of the Holy Spirit was a definite and clearly marked event at the beginning of the Christian life of the faithful. Moreover these passages must be read in the light of the typical narratives of the Acts, of 2 Tim. i. 6 f., and of Hebr. vi. 2, 4. When we thus review and coordinate all the evidence, it appears to be a safe conclusion that Confirmation was the regular practice of the Apostolic Church. It was not confined to one school of the Apostles or to one group of Churches. It had a recognised place in the life of the whole Christian society, and that from the very first. The simplest and most natural explanation of the facts lies in the belief that the Apostles knew that in this matter they were acting in accordance with the will of the Lord Himself.

From St Luke's account of the Confirmation in the city of Samaria we learn what are the two essential elements in Confirmation. The Apostles gave to the converts the outward and visible sign. From the Father in Heaven alone could there come the inward and spiritual grace; prayer was made therefore to God that He would vouchsafe the gift. In the rite of Confirmation then there *must* be (1) the prayer that the gift of the Holy Spirit may be given to those who are confirmed ; (2) the outward and visible sign of blessing. These two essential elements are preserved intact and unchanged in the Confirmation Service of the English Church.

Confirmation appears in the New Testament as distinct from, yet as closely associated with, Baptism. It is the complement of Baptism, conveying to those who have been engrafted into Christ a full participation in the divine fellowship of the regenerate life. In the records of the Apostolic age we do not possess an account of any Confirmation except in connexion with evangelistic work. Those who under these circumstances were baptised and confirmed were men and women. Questions therefore as to the separation of Baptism and Confirmation did not arise. There is no evidence in regard to the case of those who may then have been baptised as infants. We believe that the baptism of infants is required by a consideration of the essential character of Baptism. And in confirming only those who are of an age to understand the meaning of the Ordinance we believe that the Church is acting wisely in view of the essential character of Confirmation, and certainly in accordance with what we know of Apostolic practice. The decision as to the age at which those baptised in infancy shall be confirmed appears clearly to lie within the competence of a particular branch of the Catholic Church. The deviation of the practice of the later Church from the clearly recorded precedent of Apostolic times consists rather in the practice of infant baptism than in postponement of Confirmation to years of discretion. There does not appear to be any ground for thinking that the separation of Confirmation from Baptism involves any change in the character of Confirmation. Confirmation among ourselves is in regard to its essential nature precisely what Confirmation was when it was administered in the first days by the Apostles themselves.

The outward and visible sign in Confirmation was the ancient symbol of blessing, the laying on of hands. Indeed in the Apostolic Church, so far as the evidence goes, Confirmation was known as 'the laying on of hands' (Hebr. vi. 2). We found however reason to think that at least in some cases those who had been baptised, probably in addition to the imposition of hands, were anointed, this unction being a token of the fulness of the new life in the Spirit and of consecration to God.

Lastly, we ask the question What is the evidence as to the Minister of Confirmation in the Apostolic age ? Philip, the deacon and evangelist, baptises the converts at Samaria but does not confirm them. When we read of Ananias laying his hands on Saul of Tarsus that he might 'receive [his] sight and be filled with the Holy Ghost,' it is not clear that the act of Ananias was meant to be properly an act of Confirmation. If we assume that it was, it must be remembered that Ananias had received a divine command to do what he did, and that therefore the circumstances were abnormal. If then we put this narrative on one side, in each case in which the minister of Confirmation is explicitly mentioned in the New Testament, it is an Apostle. But these cases

are only three in number (Acts viii. 14 ff.,
xix. 6, 2 Tim. i. 6); and it may justly be
argued that these cases are too few to
justify the inference that no one except an
Apostle administered Confirmation in the
first age of the Church's history. Moreover it may be urged that, when the Gospel
spread widely, if Confirmation was a universal custom in the Church, its ministry
cannot have been confined to the Apostles
in the narrow sense of the word. Further,
the question which St Paul asked the
disciples whom he found at Ephesus is
significant. That question implies that he
supposed it possible that they had been
already confirmed. Now it seems certain
that St Paul was the first Apostle who
visited Ephesus; and of this he must have
been himself aware. Either then he must
have thought that these disciples had
migrated to Ephesus from some Church
where an Apostle had ministered or he
must have known that others in the Church
beside Apostles administered Confirmation. The latter alternative, though probable, is not certain. In truth the evidence
of the New Testament is too meagre to

warrant any absolute conclusion as to the Minister of Confirmation. To suppose that there was a formal and rigid rule is probably to transfer to the Apostolic age the ideas of later times. It is most likely that we shall not be far from the truth if we suppose that Confirmation was pre-eminently an Apostolic ministry, but that besides the Apostles others also who were most closely associated in position and authority with them, as for example the Prophets, were wont to lay their hands on the converts who had been baptised.

(2) Doctrinal conclusions.

The gift conveyed to the true disciple by the laying on of hands was always regarded in the Apostolic Church as nothing less than the gift of the Holy Spirit. On the day of Pentecost that Spirit was 'poured forth' on representatives of the whole Church, and henceforth the whole Church as a society was a possessor of this divine endowment. In Confirmation then the individual disciple is allowed to seek and to appropriate the gift once for all bestowed on the Body in which by Baptism he became a member. The idea of fellowship in that Body must never be allowed to recede into the background of our conception of Confirmation. In Confirmation outwardly, visibly, historically the redeemed child of God receives in its fulness the blessing which belongs to incorporation in the 'Spirit-bearing' Body of Christ. The gift which is his is not merely an inspiration or an influence of the Holy Spirit but the indwelling Presence of that divine Person who jealously yearns over those in whom He has made His abode (Jas. iv. 5) and who can be grieved by their sins, specially their sins against the unity of the Body (Eph. iv. 30).

In regard to the *past*[1]: The bestowal by God of the sanctifying Spirit is the consummation of the sentence of acquittal from the sins which have stained the past life (1 Cor. vi. 11, Tit. iii. 5).

In regard to the *present*: The gift of the Spirit is the means and evidence of adoption. The Spirit inspires the prayers

---

[1] In this paragraph and in those which follow I have adduced only those passages of the New Testament which have been discussed in the preceding pages. Other passages will readily occur to the student of the New Testament.

of the child of God (Gal. iv. 6, Rom. viii.
15). He is the seal which God sets on
those whom He makes His possession
(2 Cor. i. 22, Eph. i. 13, iv. 30) and is consequently the pledge to them of security.
Through Him there comes the consciousness of God's love (Rom. v. 5) and the
assurance that the Father Himself abides
in His redeemed child (1 John iii. 24,
iv. 13). He hallows (1 Thess. iv. 7,
2 Thess. ii. 13, 1 Cor. vi. 11) and continually renews (Tit. iii. 5 f.). He imparts
the gifts of refreshment (1 Cor. xii. 13),
joy (1 Thess. i. 6), power, love, and that
disciplined mind which gives seemliness
and moral beauty to the outward life
(2 Tim. i. 7). He unfolds the manifold
meaning of God's supreme gift in Christ
(1 Cor. ii. 12, 1 John ii. 21, 27).

In regard to the *future*: The Spirit is
the pledge of spiritual gifts which shall be
hereafter manifested (2 Cor. i. 21 f., v. 5,
Eph. i. 14) and of the 'inheritance' which
in the life of the world to come the redeemed shall have in and with Christ
(Gal. iv. 6 f., Rom. viii. 17, Titus iii. 7).

It will be observed that in the habitual

teaching of the Apostles the thought of extraordinary *charismata* has a quite subordinate place. They were not of the essence, they were the accidents, of the Pentecostal gift. They might (Acts xix. 6 ; comp. ii. 4, x. 46) or they might not (viii. 17 ; comp. ix. 17) be an evidence of the presence of the Spirit. When the Lord on the night of the betrayal explained to the Apostles what should be the office and the work of the Paraclete, He was silent in regard to them. The Apostles consistently and continually dwelt on those gifts of grace and power which through the Spirit are the permanent endowment of those who are 'in Christ.' The gift of the Spirit verily and in deed received by the faithful in Confirmation covers, it will be seen, the whole field of life and in its potency and promise reaches on into the unknown and unimagined future. It is at once an endowment and a foretaste.

God's dealings with individuals, like His dealings with the world, take the form of historical events ; such is our conclusion from a study of the Apostolic history and teaching. The great gifts of redemption are assured and conveyed in the faithful use of outward and visible signs at definite times, to which men can look back as days of regeneration and endowment. Thus our Christian position depends not on ever-changing emotions but on historical facts which must be progressively realized in life as God works in us and as we yield ourselves to His working. But it is needful for us to be jealously on our guard lest we allow ourselves to regard the Sacraments and kindred Ordinances of grace as limiting and confining our conception of God's immediate dealings with the spirits which He has made and redeemed; lest we permit phrases and formulae, hallowed by immemorial use, to become for us the final and absolute expression of God's inscrutable ways. We say, for example, as we believe that the Apostles said, that God gave the Holy Spirit to His redeemed child when with prayer he received the laying on of hands, and that now it rests with him continually to keep alive the gift once for all given to him. Such language is relatively true. It sets forth the reality of the divine gift and the duty of him who has received it to believe in it and to use it. But from another and a yet higher point of view we speak, as we believe that the Apostles spoke, of God's continual supply of the Holy Spirit, of an ever fresh gift, to use St John's pregnant phrase, of 'grace for grace.' All human language is tentative and inadequate, presenting complementary aspects of realities which essentially belong to the divine and eternal order. Again, as the history of Cornelius assures us, God works in the spirits of men in ways transcending the ordered sequence of outward ordinances, which yet we believe to be in accordance with His revealed will. The means of grace are channels which convey but do not circumscribe the bounty of God. The most convinced loyalty to the sacramental order of Christ's Holy Catholic Church is quite compatible with, nay ultimately requires, an eager and joyful recognition of the presence and of the activity of the Holy Spirit in those who refuse to seek God's gift in ways which, we are assured, have the sanction of the Apostles of Christ, and which experience from the first days until now has shewn to be valid and secure and to be full of the richest spiritual blessing.

The conclusions which we have reached as to the place of Confirmation in the Apostolic age have an important bearing on a very practical subject—the preparation of candidates for Confirmation. That preparation is of two kinds—general and special.

There must be a general preparation The Church of England plainly and with obvious wisdom requires that every one who is confirmed shall have been instructed in the rudiments of Christian belief and in the great rules of Christian conduct. Of such elementary teaching the Catechism is at once the symbol and the manual. This knowledge is a necessary prerequisite for Confirmation.

But there must also be a special preparation. If the bestowal of the outward and visible sign is not to be a bare and profitless ceremony, the candidate must understand what is the inward and spiritual grace. This is the essence of a true preparation for Confirmation. The candidate must be taught what the manifold gifts and graces of the Holy Spirit are, and what is his need of them, if he is worthily to live the life of God's redeemed child on earth. He must be taught as His child to ask the Father in Heaven to give to *him* the Holy Spirit. He must be taught the life-long duty of ever kindling afresh the gift of grace which will be in him by the laying on of hands, that he may increase in the Holy Spirit more and more until he come unto the everlasting kingdom. In all this the shepherd of souls will endeavour to follow the example of the Chief Shepherd. The Lord Himself in the upper room on the eve of the Passion and when He manifested Himself after the Resurrection prepared His disciples for the day of Pentecost. He unfolded to them the nature and office of the Paraclete. He taught them to desire and to expect 'the promise of the Father.' 'When the day of Pentecost was fully come,' they were such that on them God could 'pour forth' the gift of the Holy Spirit. Confirmation is the Pentecost of the individual soul.

ADDITIONAL NOTE ON THE MEANING OF
THE ANARTHROUS πνεῦμα, πνεῦμα ἅγιον.

What is the difference between the phrases
τὸ πνεῦμα, τὸ ἅγιον πνεῦμα, τὸ πνεῦμα τὸ ἅγιον
and on the other hand the phrases πνεῦμα,
πνεῦμα ἅγιον? The answer commonly given
to this question is to the effect that the former
group of phrases denotes the personal Holy
Spirit, the latter an operation, a gift, or an influence of the Holy Spirit. This is substantially
the view which is taken e.g, by Bishop Westcott
on John vii. 39, Dr Hort on 1 Peter i. 12, Dr
Vaughan on Hebr. ii. 4, and Dr Swete on Mark i.
8. It was apparently first formulated by Bishop
Middleton in his treatise on *The Doctrine of the
Greek Article applied to the criticism and illustra-
tion of the New Testament.* The Bishop sets
forth his conclusions in his note on Matthew i. 18
(pp. 124 ff., ed. Rose). He traces six meanings of
the word πνεῦμα, with two only of which are we
now concerned. They are these: (*a*) The word
πνεῦμα 'is employed κατ᾽ ἐξοχήν to denote the
Great and Pre-eminent Spirit, the Third Person
in the Trinity; and in this acceptation it is
worthy of remark that πνεῦμα or πνεῦμα ἅγιον
is never anarthrous; except, indeed, when other
terms, confessedly the most definite, lose the
Article from some cause alleged in the Pre-

liminary Inquiry[1].' (*b*) 'The [next] sense of
πνεῦμα is easily deducible from the [last]; being
here not the Person of the Holy Spirit but his
influence or operation…. And in this meaning
a remarkable difference may be observed with
respect to the Article. Though the Holy Spirit
be but one, his influences and operations may be
many: hence πνεῦμα and πνεῦμα ἅγιον are, in
this sense, always anarthrous, the case of *renewed
mention* or other reference being of course ex-
cepted. The expressions of "being filled with
the Holy Ghost," "receiving the Holy Ghost,"
" the Holy Ghost being upon one," &c. justify
this observation.'

There are few subtler questions of language
than the significance of the presence and of the
absence of the definite article; few so incapable
of being brought under quite definite and rigid
rules. This is preeminently the case with Greek.
The special question under consideration is
further complicated by the fact that the word
πνεῦμα is less determinate than the English
' spirit.' It signifies 'wind,' 'breath,' and hence
it may approximate in meaning to our English
expression 'inspiration'; see, e.g., John iii. 8
τὸ πνεῦμα ὅπου θέλει πνεῖ, καὶ τὴν φωνὴν αὐτοῦ
ἀκούεις, καὶ οὐκ οἶδας πόθεν ἔρχεται καὶ ποῦ
ὑπάγει· οὕτως ἐστὶν πᾶς ὁ γεγεννημένος ἐκ τοῦ

---

[1] E.g. 'In propositions which merely affirm or deny existence,
the name of the person or thing, of which existence is affirmed
or denied, is without the Article' (p. 42).

πνεύματος : John xx. 22 f. ἐνεφύσησεν καὶ λέγει αὐτοῖς Λάβετε πνεῦμα ἅγιον (where it is impossible not to interpret the Lord's words in close connexion with the Lord's act): 1 Cor. xii. 10 διακρίσεις πνευμάτων : xiv. 12 ζηλωταί ἐστε πνευμάτων. Again, it is well to remember that πνεῦμα and even πνεῦμα ἅγιον may refer to the spirit of man. Thus in 2 Cor. vi. 6 (ἐν χρηστότητι, ἐν πνεύματι ἁγίῳ, ἐν ἀγάπῃ ἀνυποκρίτῳ) it seems impossible to refer the words ἐν πνεύματι ἁγίῳ to the divine Spirit; compare Susanna 45 (Theod.) ἐξήγειρεν ὁ θεὸς τὸ πνεῦμα τὸ ἅγιον παιδαρίου νεωτέρου ᾧ ὄνομα Δανιήλ. But, when every allowance has been made for elasticity and ambiguity of meaning, I find it impossible to subscribe to Bishop Middleton's canon as to the anarthrous πνεῦμα ἅγιον. The anarthrous πνεῦμα and πνεῦμα ἅγιον are, I believe, essentially capable of denoting the personal Holy Spirit. There may be, and perhaps always is, a difference of *nuance,* but the expressions πνεῦμα ἅγιον and τὸ πνεῦμα τὸ ἅγιον are substantially identical in meaning.

We must then briefly collect and review the facts (1) of the language of the Old Testament (Hebrew and Greek); (2) of the language of the New Testament.

(1) Old Testament.

In the Old Testament 'the Spirit' (הָרוּחַ, τὸ πνεῦμα) is used absolutely of the Spirit of

God. Thus Numb. xi. 25—29 'And the Lord came down in the cloud, and spake unto him, and took of the spirit that was upon him, and put it upon the seventy elders: and it came to pass, that, when the spirit rested upon them, they prophesied, but they did so no more. But there remained two men in the camp, the name of the one was Eldad, and the name of the other Medad: and the spirit rested upon them; and they were of them that were written, but had not gone out unto the Tent: and they prophesied in the camp.... And Moses said unto him, Art thou jealous for my sake? would God that all the Lord's people were prophets, that the Lord would put his spirit upon them!' From the closing words of this passage it is clear that 'the Spirit' is throughout 'the Spirit of the Lord.'

There are however several passages in which the simple anarthrous substantive— רוּחַ, 'Spirit' —is not indefinite but, like הָרוּחַ, 'the Spirit,' is used to denote the Spirit of God. They are these:

Numb. xxvii. 18 'Take thee Joshua the son of Nun, a man in whom is the spirit (רוּחַ), and lay thine hand upon him.' Comp. Gen. xli. 38 'Can we find such a one as this, a man in whom the spirit of God is?'

Isaiah xxxii. 15 'Until the spirit (רוּחַ)

be poured upon us from on high.' Comp. Ezek. xxxix. 29 'I have poured out my spirit upon the house of Israel, saith the Lord God,' Joel ii. 28, Prov. i. 23.

Ezek. ii. 2 'And the spirit (רוּחַ) entered into me when he spake unto me.' The first clause is repeated in iii. 24. Comp. e.g. Numb. xxiv. 2 'And the spirit of God came upon him,' Judg. iii. 10, 1 Sam. x. 6, 10, 2 Chron. xv. 1.

Ezek. iii. 12 'Then the spirit (רוּחַ) lifted me up.' So viii. 3, xi. 1, 24, xliii. 5. Comp. xxxvii. 1 'The hand of the Lord was upon me and he carried me out in the spirit of the Lord.'

1 Chron. xii. 18 'Then the spirit (רוּחַ) clothed Amasai.' Comp. Judg. vi. 34 'The spirit of the Lord clothed Gideon,' 2 Chron. xxiv. 20 'The spirit of God clothed Zechariah.'

The omission of the Article with 'Spirit' in these passages probably comes under the general grammatical statement 'In prose also the Article is omitted with expressions familiar' (Davidson *Hebrew Syntax* § 22, (*e*), Rem. 3). But, whatever the explanation may be, the fact seems to be established that the anarthrous רוּחַ 'Spirit,' in a series of passages in the Old Testament is used as a designation of the divine Spirit. We are not now concerned with the theological question as to the meaning in the Old Testament of the words 'the Spirit of God' and the like.

For the interpretation of the New Testament it is even more important to notice the usage of the LXX[1]. In all these passages quoted just above the anarthrous רוּחַ is represented in the LXX. by the anarthrous πνεῦμα[2]. To these passages may be added Numb. xi. 26 καὶ ἐπανεπαύσατο ἐπ᾽ αὐτοὺς πνεῦμα (Codd. AF τὸ πνεῦμα)—a passage the more remarkable since in the previous verse we have the phrase ὡς δὲ ἐπανεπαύσατο τὸ πνεῦμα ἐπ᾽ αὐτούς.

(2) New Testament.

The language which the writers of the New Testament used as to the Holy Spirit was an inheritance from the Church of Israel. We should expect therefore to find instances in the New Testament of the anarthrous πνεῦμα, πνεῦμα ἅγιον, employed as synonymous with τὸ πνεῦμα, τὸ πνεῦμα τὸ ἅγιον. I propose (i) to review certain passages in which the anarthrous πνεῦμα or πνεῦμα ἅγιον is used and the context appears to define the meaning; (ii) to examine certain phrases.

(i) I take first a passage—Acts xix. 2 ff.— to which frequent reference has been made in the preceding pages. St Paul when he arrived at

---

[1] It may possibly be suggested that in these passages an original אֱלֹהִים (יהוה) has dropped out after רוּחַ. If this was the case, the omission was early enough to affect the LXX. and (through the LXX.) the New Testament.

[2] In Numb. xxvii. 18 a corrector of Cod. Ambrosianus (Cod. F) seems to read πνεῦμα θεοῦ.

Ephesus asked certain disciples whom he found there the question εἰ πνεῦμα ἅγιον ἐλάβετε πιστεύσαντες; It is probable that St Paul is St Luke's immediate authority for the narrative and that the words represent St Paul's own remembrance of what was actually said. We cannot however assume this as a certainty; the phrases may be due to the historian. Did the historian then (whether St Paul was his authority or not) mean to represent the Apostle as asking the Ephesian disciples whether they had received the Holy Ghost Himself or whether they had received a χάρισμα πνευματικόν, a gift of the Holy Ghost? The subsequent history appears to leave us in no doubt as to the meaning of the Apostle's question. When the disciples answered in the negative, the Apostle instructed them. They were baptised. He laid his hands on them and 'the Holy Ghost came on them (ἦλθε τὸ πνεῦμα τὸ ἅγιον ἐπ' αὐτούς).' The historian wrote verse 2 —St Paul's question—in full knowledge of the sequel which he was just about to record. The subsequent history interprets the question. The τὸ πνεῦμα τὸ ἅγιον in verse 6 fixes the meaning of the πνεῦμα ἅγιον in verse 2.

Again, in 1 Cor. ii. 12 St Paul says that 'we received the spirit which is from God (τὸ πνεῦμα τὸ ἐκ τοῦ θεοῦ); that we might know the things that are freely given to us by God.' He then continues ἃ καὶ λαλοῦμεν οὐκ ἐν διδακτοῖς ἀνθρωπίνης σοφίας λόγοις, ἀλλ' ἐν διδακτοῖς πνεύματος.

The καί—ἃ καὶ λαλοῦμεν—emphasises the close correspondence between the knowledge of Christian truth and the proclamation of Christian truth. The same Spirit who teaches the truth teaches the words in which that truth may be appropriately expressed. The reference in the phrase ἐν διδακτοῖς πνεύματος is defined by the preceding words ἐλάβομεν...τὸ πνεῦμα τὸ ἐκ τοῦ θεοῦ.

Again, in 1 Cor. xii. 3 St Paul asserts οὐδεὶς ἐν πνεύματι θεοῦ λαλῶν λέγει Ἀνάθεμα Ἰησοῦς, καὶ οὐδεὶς δύναται εἰπεῖν Κύριος Ἰησοῦς εἰ μὴ ἐν πνεύματι ἁγίῳ. Does he here refer to ' an inspiration from God ' and to ' a holy inspiration ' or to the personal Holy Spirit? The succeeding context shews decisively that the latter is the true answer. For he continues ' Now there are diversities of gifts, but the same Spirit (τὸ δὲ αὐτὸ πνεῦμα).' That the last words can only point in the fullest sense to the personal Holy Spirit is clear from the two parallel phrases, ' the same Lord,' ' the same God.' The Apostle then goes on to draw out the thought of the distribution of the gifts of the one Spirit. ' To each one is given the manifestation of the Spirit to profit withal.... All these [operations] worketh the one and the same Spirit, dividing to each one severally even as he will.' If any lingering doubt remains whether St Paul is thinking of an influence or gift of the Spirit, or on the other hand of the divine Person, it is removed by the concluding words 'even as he will.' Further, in the enumeration of the manifold gifts of the one Spirit 'faith' has a place; 'to another faith in the same Spirit (ἐν τῷ αὐτῷ πνεύματι).' In these words, which do not admit of doubt, we have a comment on the phrases under discussion ἐν πνεύματι θεοῦ, ἐν πνεύματι ἁγίῳ. The particular expression πίστις ἐν τῷ αὐτῷ πνεύματι as well as the context as a whole shew conclusively that the absence of the definite article does not imply any indefiniteness in the phrases ἐν πνεύματι θεοῦ, ἐν πνεύματι ἁγίῳ: they can only be interpreted of the one divine Person, the Holy Spirit.

(ii) The same conclusion is reached if we examine particular phrases.

In Acts ii. 4 we read ἐπλήσθησαν πάντες πνεύματος ἁγίου καὶ ἤρξαντο λαλεῖν ἑτέραις γλώσσαις: in iv. 8 Πέτρος πλησθεὶς πνεύματος ἁγίου εἶπεν πρὸς αὐτούς κ.τ.λ. But in iv. 31 (where there has been no allusion in the preceding context which can account for the presence of the article) we read ἐπλήσθησαν ἅπαντες τοῦ ἁγίου πνεύματος, καὶ ἐλάλουν τὸν λόγον τοῦ θεοῦ μετὰ παρρησίας. Again, we have the phrase ἐν δυνάμει πνεύματος ἁγίου (Rom. xv. 13, 19) but elsewhere (Luke iv. 14) ἐν τῇ δυνάμει τοῦ πνεύματος, while the idea receives full and unambiguous expression in our Lord's words (Acts i. 8) λήμψεσθε δύναμιν ἐπελθόντος τοῦ ἁγίου πνεύματος ἐφ' ὑμᾶς. Again, in Phil. ii. 1 St Paul uses the phrase κοινωνία πνεύματος, but in 2 Cor. xiii. 13 ἡ κοινωνία τοῦ ἁγίου πνεύματος. Lastly, we take the expression, the crucial expression in connexion with Confirmation, λαβεῖν πνεῦμα ἅγιον (Acts viii. 15, 17, 19; xix. 2); elsewhere however the article is prefixed to πνεῦμα—Acts x. 47 τὸ πνεῦμα τὸ ἅγιον ἔλαβον, 1 Cor. ii. 12 ἐλάβομεν ...τὸ πνεῦμα τὸ ἐκ τοῦ θεοῦ, Gal. iii. 2 τὸ πνεῦμα ἐλάβετε (comp. John vii. 39); and in Acts ii. 38 a still more emphatic phrase is employed λήμψεσθε τὴν δωρεὰν τοῦ ἁγίου πνεύματος (comp. Acts x. 45, Phil. i. 19, 1 John iii. 24, iv. 13).

A consideration of these passages and of these synonymous phrases requires, I believe, the conclusion that the anarthrous πνεῦμα, πνεῦμα ἅγιον, is capable of expressing clearly and definitely the Holy Spirit in the full personal sense.

The question remains what explanation can be given of this definite use of the anarthrous πνεῦμα, πνεῦμα ἅγιον. The explanation is to be found in the recognition of two principles. (1) The phrases τὸ πνεῦμα τὸ ἅγιον, τὸ ἅγιον πνεῦμα, τὸ πνεῦμα, πνεῦμα ἅγιον, πνεῦμα have come to have the character of proper names and hence without alteration of essential meaning the article may or may not be prefixed. (2) The omission of the article before a substantive in many cases does not imply indefiniteness but lays stress on character; it is qualitative. Thus Hebr. i. 2 ἐπ᾽ ἐσχάτου τῶν ἡμερῶν τούτων ἐλάλησεν ἡμῖν ἐν υἱῷ, i.e. 'in Him who is nothing less than the Son'; xii. 7 τίς γὰρ υἱὸς ὃν οὐ παιδεύει πατήρ, i.e. 'one who bears to him the unique relation of father.' This is the significance of the anarthrous πνεῦμα, πνεῦμα ἅγιον in very many passages. When, for example, a writer is insisting on a contrast, he dwells on character and omits the article. Thus when baptism with the Spirit is contrasted with baptism with water (e.g. Mark i. 8, Acts i. 5) or when the Spirit is set over against the flesh (e.g. Rom. viii. 4, 9, 13) the anarthrous πνεῦμα or πνεῦμα ἅγιον is used. This seems to be the explanation of the phrase ἐν διδακτοῖς πνεύματος (1 Cor. ii. 13; see above pp. 125 f.). It must be added that these two principles are not mutually exclusive but may coincide in their operation. Take the word θεός, which, like πνεῦμα ἅγιον, is a quasi-proper name. The anarthrous θεός is often used to call emphatic attention to the fact that no one inferior to God Himself is spoken of. In the phrase ὃς ἐν μορφῇ θεοῦ ὑπάρχων (Phil. ii. 6), if we substitute τοῦ θεοῦ for θεοῦ, we feel at once how much less forcible the words become. Or replace θεόν by τὸν θεόν in the phrases θεὸν οὐδεὶς ἑώρακεν πώποτε (John i. 18), θεὸν οὐδεὶς πώποτε τεθέαται (1 John iv. 12); and we are conscious that the sentences are robbed of their peculiar and arresting vigour: the order of the words and the omission of the article here combine to emphasize θεόν. The same is true of the word χριστός. In 1 Cor. i. 23 (ἡμεῖς δὲ κηρύσσομεν χριστὸν ἐσταυρωμένον) how much depends on the absence of the article? The thought is concentrated on the paradox—'the one who is anointed of God yet crucified by man.' In the same way, especially if we read the language of the Apostles aloud and become aware of its subtle feeling, we shall discover that when the anarthrous πνεῦμα and πνεῦμα ἅγιον are used the intention of the writer is to dwell on the unique character of Him of whom he speaks. The absence of the article is a means of emphasis.

We take as an example John vii. 39 τοῦτο δὲ εἶπεν περὶ τοῦ πνεύματος οὗ ἔμελλον λαμβάνειν οἱ πιστεύσαντες εἰς αὐτόν· οὔπω γὰρ ἦν πνεῦμα, ὅτι Ἰησοῦς οὔπω ἐδοξάσθη. Here the second clause (γάρ) explains the ἔμελλον of the first. It seems to follow that the τὸ πνεῦμα of the first clause and the πνεῦμα of the second are co-extensive in meaning. The apparent difficulty in the way of this interpretation really lies in the words οὔπω ἦν, which superficially may be regarded as denying the existence of the Holy Spirit before Pentecost. The meaning however of the expression is sufficiently defined by the preceding context; the οὔπω ἦν must be interpreted in the light of the ἔμελλον λαμβάνειν. The best comment on οὔπω ἦν...ἐδοξάσθη is John xvi. 7 ἐὰν γὰρ μὴ ἀπέλθω, ὁ παράκλητος οὐ μὴ ἔλθῃ πρὸς ὑμᾶς (comp. xiv. 26, xvi. 13). The anarthrous πνεῦμα lays stress on the essential idea of πνεῦμα and can best be represented in English simply by an emphasis on the word Spirit—'the *Spirit*,' there being an implied contrast between 'the Spirit' and the Lord 'not yet glorified' but still 'known' by men 'after the flesh.'

INDEX

133

INDEX

CAMBRIDGE : PRINTED BY JOHN CLAY, M.A. AT THE UNIVERSITY PRESS.

www.ingramcontent.com/pod-product-compliance
Lightning Source LLC
Chambersburg PA
CBHW060353090426
42734CB00011B/2130